MOMMY'S

CLASSROOM CURRICULUM

Priscilla Morales

Printed in the United States of America

ISBN: 9798693525085

10 9 8 7 6 5 4 3 2 1

EMPIRE PUBLISHING

www.empirebookpublishing.com

Introduction

Welcome to Mommy's Classroom a curriculum designed to create an effective and flexible home learning environment. I am so excited to be joining you and your child on this homeschool journey! As both a teacher and a mother, I understand the importance of establishing a strong educational foundation for early learners. This curriculum is based on early childhood education state standards, and this mother's desire to help children thrive both inside and outside of an educational setting.

One of the things that I learned very early on in my career as a teacher is that my mindset plays a crucial role in the way in which I convey information to my students. If you are excited about learning and creating fun activities, then your child will be more inclined to participate. It's all about attitude my friend. Personally, I am in no way shape or form ready to teach before my morning coffee! There is no way that I will be able to keep it peppy and fun, if I have not taken care of myself. So, make sure that you, yourself, are ready to begin. Ask yourself, what do you need to start this lesson with the right mindset? Is it coffee? Prayer? Yoga? Whatever it is, do it before you begin! Teaching is waaaaay more fun when you are fully engaged in the lesson plan!

One of the best parts of homeschooling is the flexibility of when, where, and how you will incorporate your lesson plans. For me, morning hours work best for my schedule. After breakfast our kitchen table, living room, couch, and backyard become our learning environment. You choose when and where you think your child will be more focused and better able to complete each lesson.

Once you have decided whether you are a morning, noon, or evening teacher establish a pre-lesson routine so that your daily transition into learning time will be easier and without hiccups. Morning lessons work best for me. After breakfast, I give my son about 15 minutes of free play. This allows him the opportunity to burn off some energy, which will help to keep him calm and focused for our learning activity. During this time, I set up for our circle time. Once the morning learning songs starts playing my son knows that it is time for school. I found the song transition to be much more pleasant than me yelling "Sit down for school!" Once he sits down for circle time, I reward him with a super star sticker. Positive reinforcement for good behavior is essential in helping children to stay actively engaged in the lesson. I created a happy face chart to visually help my son with positive reinforcement. If my son earns more happy faces than sad faces then he will get a treat at the end of the session. I try to keep it healthy so his treat is usually an apple sauce snack or an orange with a silly face drawn on it. One day he will figure out that mom was hoarding the candy stash instead of sharing, but until then he is happy with silly faced fruit!

Another factor that can mean the difference between a smooth lesson and a pouty lesson is preparation! It is important to do your best in preparing the learning material beforehand. If the lesson requires cotton balls, strips of paper, or colors have them all ready to go! Early learners are quick to shift focus so you want to do your very best to keep them on task. This is easier done when you don't have to run to the closet or pantry to grab extra materials. If you shift focus then your little ones are likely to do the same. I should know. The moment I venture out of sight I hear the pitter patter of little feet followed by "Mom, what are you doing? Usually this is when I'm in the bathroom!

One of the reasons I love homeschooling is because it is so time flexible. It all depends on your child. Each day is different. I strive for ten to fifteen minutes rotations between activities. This works well for my three-year-old. However, some days we will spend a considerable amount of time on a particular activity, this is especially true if I see that he is really engaged. If I see that he is becoming frustrated or distracted I may shorten the time. When this happens, I usually attempt to revisit the particular activity later or I modify it to fit the needs of my son. For example, if the activity calls for finger painting and my son is reluctant to get his fingers dipped in paint, then I'll use a paintbrush instead. If he has not mastered the previous week's number, I might have him review that number instead of moving on to the current number of the week. Remember the lesson is plan is a convenient guideline, but I encourage you to modify the lesson so that it fits the individual needs of your child. Over the years I prepared countless lesson plans, but I always allowed room for flexibility. Each child is unique in their learning. They absorb and store information at their own pace. Some students are visual learners, others are auditory learners, and some thrive when given the opportunity to learn through hands on activities. The trick to being a great teacher is to implement lessons that will allow students to learn in a manner that is most beneficial to them. Let's get started! Welcome to the homeschool squad!

Assessments:

A great way to see your child's academic progress is through the use of a portfolio. You will begin to track your child's learning progress on the very first day of home school. The following pages will contain assessments that will give your insight into your child's academic starting point. You will administer the assessments in the beginning, middle, and end of the year. This will help you to customize each lesson to meet your child's individual needs.

Make 3 Copies of the following assessments:

Name: Date:

Does he/she know her ABC Song   Yes   No   Notes:

Can he/she identify the letters of the alphabet by sight?   Yes   No   Notes:

What is the highest number that he/she can count to without help?   Number:

                                                                                    Notes
:

Is he/she able to match upper case with lower case letters?

Yes   No   Able to match only some Which Ones?

Is he/she able to identify primary colors?   Yes   No   Partial

Name: Date:

Does he/she know her ABC Song?	Yes	No	Partial Notes:
Can he/she identify the letters of the Alphabet by sight?	Yes	No	Notes:
What is the highest number that he/she can count to without help?	Number:		Notes:
Is he/she able to match upper case with lower case letters?	Yes	No	Able to match only some: Which Ones?
Is he/she able to identify primary colors?	Yes	No	Partial Notes:
Does he/she understand the concept of adding and subtracting?	Yes	No	

Aa	Bb	Cc	Dd	
Ee	Ff	Gg	Hh	
Ii	Jj	Kk	Ll	
Mm	Nn	Oo	Pp	
Qq	Rr	Ss	Tt	
Uu	Vv	Ww	Xx	
Yy	Zz			

Identify each letter

Present different colored items to your child (EX) Counting Blocks, Crayons, Legos, etc.

Child's Name:	Age:	Date
What Color is it?	**Mastered (X)**	**Needs Work (X)**

Child's Name: **Date:**

Mark the numbers that your child can identify by sight. Skip around to different numbers.

1	2	3	4	5	6	7	8	9	10
11	12	13	14	15	16	17	18	19	20
21	22	23	24	25	26	27	28	29	30
31	32	33	34	35	36	37	38	39	40
41	42	43	44	45	46	47	48	49	50
51	52	53	54	55	56	57	58	59	60
61	62	63	64	65	66	67	68	69	70
71	72	73	74	75	76	77	78	79	80
81	82	83	84	85	86	87	88	89	90
91	92	92	94	95	96	97	98	99	100

Child's Name: Date:

Place the assessments inside your portfolio. One of the most gratifying things about teaching is seeing your students' progress at the end of the year.

Circle Time:

What is it? It's the time when you review or introduce new learning material. So, I set up a colorful rug. After we have some morning free play, I play the "Clean Up" song. He knows it is time to put his toys away and to gather on the carpet. We sit down and sing our daily learning songs, which include ABCs, days of the week, and months of the year song. First, we sing our ABC song. After the song I introduce or review the letter of the week! You can use a whiteboard or a letter card to show your child the letter! I have used both! My son loves to participate so I'll let him hold the card, or circle the letter on the white board! Keep them involved.

After the letter of the week we sing our days of the week and months of the year song. This is the time when we bring out our special interactive calendar. After Calendar time we review our color, through song and dance. Finally, we read a book related to the theme, but any book that they are showing interests in will do!

Materials Needed for Circle Time:

Kid friendly calendar

I purchased a magnetic calendar that displays the days, months, and seasons of the year. You definitely don't have to purchase one you can totally use any kid friendly calendar as long as you have a visual to go along with the singing to help them to develop a better understanding of concept of days and months you are good to go! It also helps with developing early literary skills.

ABC Chart: I made my own chart! Poster board and markers are great!

A lot of the learning your child will do will be through song and play. I make it a point to incorporate a lot of music in our circle time. I found it extremely helpful in aiding my son's intellectual development. You have a choice of downloading your favorite versions of academic songs, or simply singing them yourself. I do a combo of both.

These are some of the songs that I have chosen for my circle time. I downloaded them from **Amazon Music.** However, you can choose to download your own version of each song, or you can simply choose to sing your songs acapella. Whatever works best for you!

Days of the Week Song: Dream English Best of Kids Songs Volume2

ABC Song: Muffin Songs Children Hit Songs Vol.1 Lesson One!

What Color are You Wearing? The Kiboomers

The Months of the Year: The Kiboomers

I always read a book during circle time. These books are simply a guide in case you are looking for recommendations for the given theme. However, feel free to read any book you think your child will enjoy. You do not have to purchase these books you can check them out at your local library.

All About Me Theme:

I like myself by Karen Beaumont

Marvelous Me by Lisa Marie Bullard

What I like About Me! : A Book Celebrating Differences by Allia Zobel Nolan

Feelings and Behavior Books:

Hands are Not for Hitting by Martine Agassi

Voices are Not for Yelling by Elizabeth Verdick

Words are Not for Hurting by Elizabeth Verdic

Fall Theme:

Biscuit Visits the Pumpkin Patch by Alyssa Satin Capucilli

Thanksgiving Parade by Kelly Asbury

Mouse's First Fall by Lauren Thompson

Peek –A Who? By Nina Laden

Christmas Theme

The Itsy Bitsy Reindeer by Jeffrey Burton

Christmas in the Manger by Nola Buck

How to Catch an Elf by Adam Wallace

Construction Site on Christmas Night by Sherri Duskey Rinker

Artic theme

Sneezy the Snowman by Maureen Wright

Hello World! Artic Animals by Jill McDonald

Polar Animals by Wade Cooper

Artic Animals (Who's That?) by Tad Carpenter

Valentine's Day Theme:

Llamma Llamma I love you by Anna Dewney

Love Monster by Rachel Bright

My Fuzzy Valentine by Naomi Kleinberg

Hug Machine by Scott Campbell

Farm Animal Theme

Barnyard Dance by Sandra Boynton

Farm Animals by Pheobe Dunn

The Little Red Hen by Carol Ottonlenghi

Old MacDonald Had a Farm by Little Hippo Books

Sheep in a Jeep by Nancy E. Shaw

Ocean Theme:

Smile Pout- Pout Fish by Deborah Diesen

The Rainbow Fish by Marcus Pfister

National Geographic kids Look and Learn: Ocean Creatures by National Geographic Kids

Guess Who Ocean Friends by Jodie Shepherd

Bug Theme:

The Itsy Bitsy Pumpkin by Sonali Fry

The Very Busy Spider by Eric Carle

The Grouchy Lady Bug by Eric Carle

The backyard Bug Book for Kids: Storybook, Insect Facts, and Activities by Lauren Davidson

The Very Hungry Caterpillar by Eric Carle

Weather Books:

National Geographic Kids little Kids First board Book: Weather by Ruth A. Muscrave

Rain, Rain, Go Away by Caroline Jayne Church

National Geographic Kids look and Learn: Look Outside! (Look&Learn)

Freddy the Frogcaster by Janice Dean

Colors and Shapes

Brown Bear, Brown Bear, What Do You See? By Bill Martin Jr/Eric Carle

Shapes by Scholastic

Craft Materials to stalk up on:

Multicolor construction paper

Regular white print paper Crayons

Washable paint

Child Friendly scissors Markers

Tissue gift paper
Empty sensory bottles
Fuzzy multicolor pom poms
Glitter glue
Glitter Baby oil

Sensory Bin:

A plastic bin large enough to fit 3 pairs of shoes (think work boots).

Portfolio:

3 Ring Binder, dividers, and sheet protectors. I love using portfolios because it allows me to keep track of my child's academic progress. Designate one section of your portfolio specifically for your assessments. Designate another section to collect activities that require your child to display their writing and drawing skills, designate another section for tracking their skills in shape and number recognition. Place the activities themselves, or pictures of the activities in the designated sections of
the portfolio. This will allow you to keep track of your child's learning throughout the year.

Section 1: Assessments

Section 2: Writing and Drawing Section

3: Numbers and Shapes

All about Me Theme: Week 1

	Circle Time	Craft	Sensory	Gross Motor	Fine Motor	Materials Needed
Monday	Letter of the Week: Aa Number of the Week :1 Color of the Week: Red Shape of the Week: Circle Your Choice Book	Craft Self Portrait Place your child in front of a mirror. Give them a choice of crayons or washable markers. Have them draw their self-portrait!	Sensory Bin Fill your bin with the following: -water -plastic scoops -plastic bowls - add a few drops of red food coloring to the water	Dance Party! Put on your child's favorite dance music! Join them in a fun dance party!	Noodle Necklaces! Give your child a long strand of yarn and some rigatoni pasta! Have your child lace the yarn through the pasta to create a necklace. Help them to tie the ends together when they are done lacing!	Self Portrait: -print paper -mirror -crayons/washable markers Sensory Bin -plastic container large enough to fit 3 pairs of shoes. -plastic scoops -plastic bowls -water -red food coloring NOTE: Always supervise your child when playing with water or small objects that may pose

						choking hazard. Noodle Necklace -rigatoni pasta -yarn
Tuesday	Letter of the Week: Aa Number of the Week :1 Color of the Week: Red Shape of the Week : Circle Your Choice Book	Cheerio Circles! Use a black marker to draw a large circle on a piece of red construction paper. The circle should be in the center of the paper and should take up at least half of the paper. Give your child a plastic bowl full of cheerios and some glue. Have them trace the circle with glue, and then add on	Shaving Cream Fun! Place a plastic mat on your table. Add a blob of shaving cream to the center! Have your child use their hands to move the shaving cream around! Have them draw some circles and practice writing the letter Aa with their finger!	Letter Hop Using side walk chalk write down the Letter Aa at least 5 times. Spread them out to give your child room to hop from Aa to Aa	Red 1 Give your child some red tissue paper. Have them tear the paper into small pieces. Using a black marker, write down the number 1 in multiple locations on a white piece of print paper (at least 10 times). Have your child glue the torn pieces of tissue paper to each of	Cheerio Circles: -red construction paper -glue -black marker Cheerios/Fruit Honey O's (any kind of cereal that is the shape of a circle will work. Shaving Cream Fun! -Shaving Cream -plastic table mat Aa! Aa! Aa! -Sidewalk Chalk

		some cheerios also known as mini circles!			the numbers! Have your child say the number out loud as they glue on the tissue paper.	If you are indoors write the letter Aa down on some regular print paper and tape it securely to the ground! Red 1 -red tissue paper -white print paper -black marker -glue
Wednesday	Letter of the Week: Aa Number of the Week :1 Color of the Week: Red Shape of the Week: Circle Your Choice Book!	Red Apple Stamp! Cut an apple in half and give it to your child. Give your child some red washable paint. Have your child stamp the now flat side of their apple onto the paint	Sensory Bin Fill your sensory bin with: -kinetic sand -plastic scoops -toy trucks	Catch the Circle! Find a big bouncy child friendly ball and play a game of catch the circle!	Build a Play Dough Family! Have your child build their play dough family! Questions to ask: How many sisters/brothers do you have?	Red Apple Stamp! -white construction paper -red washable paint -apple Sensory Bin: -plastic bin large enough to

		and then onto a white piece of construction paper multiple times!			What type of games do you like to play with them? What's your mama's name? What type of activities do you like to do with mama?	fit 3 pairs of shoes -Kinetic Sand (You can add scoops/toy trucks/anything to make it extra fun). Catch the Circle: Kid friendly Ball Play Dough Family: -play dough (You can buy or make your own).
Thursday	Letter of the Week: Aa Number of the Week :1 Color of the Week: Red Shape of the Week: Circle Your Choice Book	Craft: Decorate the number by finger painting! Using a black marker draw the number 1 on a white construction paper. It should be at least half of the size of the paper.	Salt Tray: Fill a tray or paper plate with some salt! Have your child practice writing the letter "Aa" with their finger.	Gross Motor Skip across the room or back yard with your child! As you are skipping count to ten out loud!	Fine Motor Cotton Ball Clean Up! Give your child some cotton balls and an empty plastic bowl. Have them use child friendly tweezers to place the cotton balls	Red Fingerprints -black marker -white construction paper -red washable finger-paint Salt Pan Activity: -Flat container (paper

		Have your child dip their finger in some red finger-paint and trace the number 1 by leaving their fingerprint all along the lines of the number.			in the plastic bowl.	plates work great!) -Salt -Number Line Skip to 10 my darling! Just yourselves! Cotton Ball Clean Up!
Friday	Letter of the Week: Aa Number of the Week: 1 Color of the Week: Red Shape of the Week: Circle Your Choice Book!	Family Portrait Give your child a picture of your family. Have them name all of your family members. Tell them they are going to draw and paint their own family picture! Give them some -white construction paper -washable paints -paint brush	Sensory Bin Fill your bin with the following: -dry oats -plastic measuring cups -plastic funnels	Gross Motor: Balloon Tennis -ping pong paddles -red balloon	Using a black marker draw a large letter "A" on a paper plate. Using a hole puncher punch holes along the lines of the letter. Give your child a shoe lace! Have them lace the letter "A"	Family Portrait: -white construction paper -washable paints -paint brush -family picture (Set the family picture in an area far enough away so that your child doesn't get paint on it!) -Sensory Bin -plastic bin large enough to

						fit 3 pairs of shoes
						-dry oats
						-plastic funnels
						-measuring cups
						Balloon Tennis:
						-ping pong paddles
						-red balloon
						Note: If you are doing this activity outdoors inflate at least 3.
						Lacing "A"
						-shoe lace
						-hole puncher
						-black marker
						-paper plate

All About Me Unit: Week: 2

	Circle Time	Craft	Sensory	Gross Motor	Fine Motor	Materials Needed
Monday	Letter of the Week: Bb Number of the Week :2 Color of the Week: Yellow Shape of the Week: Triangle Your Choice Book!	B is for Bee Craft Give your child some black and white construction paper. Have your child tear both black and white papers into small pieces. On a white piece of construction paper draw a large letter B. It should take up at least half of the paper. Have your child glue on the construction paper to create a black and yellow pattern as	Colorful Ice cubes! Add some yellow food coloring to some water, then freeze water using 2-3 ice cube trays. Place them in your sensory bin. Add some water so the ice cubes float! Add some red food coloring to the water in the bin! -throw in some plastic cups for pouring!	High Knee Marching Play an audio recording of a marching drum beat! March around the house as you count 1-10 Keep their knees high and their arms moving.	Practice Cutting straight lines! Using a black marker and a regular sheet of print paper draw horizontal lines across the page. Give your child some kid friendly scissors and have them practice cutting along the lines.	Bee Craft: -white, black, and yellow construction paper -black marker -glue Sensory Bin: -plastic bin large enough to fit 3 pairs of shoes -red and yellow food coloring -plastic cups -water High Knee Marching -Recorded Audio of a Drum Beat Practice Cutting -print paper

		they trace the letter B.			-child friendly scissors -black marker. Or you opt to use an already printed page from your chosen activity book.
Tuesday	Letter of the Week: Bb Number of the Week: 2 Color of the Week: Yellow Shape of the Week: Triangle Your Choice Book!	Pizza Slice Craft! Using a yellow construction paper cut out a large triangle (a big pizza slice!) Precut some small triangles using red construction paper (for toppings! Make sure to cut some circles to review the previous week's lesson. Have your child glue	Toy Bubbles Bath Wash! Fill up your sensory container with bath bubbles and water. Throw in some of their favorite tub toys! (Always supervise your child when playing with water or small items)	Water Bottle Bowling Give your child a kid friendly bouncy ball! Set up some water bottles to use as bowling pins! Have a fun game of bowling!	Stickers and the Letter "B"! Using a black marker/pen a large letter B on a sheet of print paper (the letter should take up most of the paper). Give your child some fun stickers (stars, happy faces, etc.) Have them trace the lines of the letter B with their stickers!	Triangle Pizza: -Glue -yellow and red construction paper Toy Bubble Bath Wash: -plastic container large enough to fit 3 pairs of shoes -water -bath bubbles -bath toys Water Bottle Bowling:

		their toppings onto their pizza slice!				-water bottles (5) -kid friendly ball Stickers and The Letter "B" -print paper -black marker/pen -fun stickers (stars, happy faces, etc.)
Wednesday	Letter of the Week: Bb Number of the Week :2 Color of the Week: Yellow Shape of the Week: Triangle Your choice book!	My favorite things (Handprint Craft) Using washable paint, cover inside of your child's hand yellow and stamp it onto a white construction paper. Paint the inside of their other hand in red paint (to review the previous	Sensory Bin: Fill your chosen sensory bins with fuzzy pom poms. -plastic cups -child friendly tweezers As your child is playing with the pom poms ask them how to they feel on their skin?	Bobsled Buddy Push! Fill your laundry basket with your child's favorite stuffed animals! Have them push their buddies across the room. Count from numbers 1-10 as they push their buddies	Pipe Cleaners and plastic Strainer. Have your child place the pipe cleaners in the openings of the plastic strainer for some fine motor play!	My favorite things (Handprint Craft): -white construction Paper Washable yellow, red, and child's choice color washable paint. Sensory Bin: -plastic bin large enough to fit 3 pairs of shoes

		week's lesson). Finally ask them what their favorite color is and then paint their hand using that particular color. Set it aside to dry. As the paint is drying ask them the following questions: -What's your favorite snack? What's your favorite color? What is your favorite game to play? Once their hand prints dry you can write their answers on their handprints using a		across the room!		-fuzzy pom poms -plastic cups -child friendly tweezers Note: Always supervise your child when playing with small objects that may pose choking hazards! Bobsled Buddy Push: -Stuffed Animals -Laundry Basket (Note if you are doing this activity on a smooth surface, I recommend placing a towel beneath the basket to make it easier to push. It will also help to prevent

		black marker!				floor scratches. Make sure to use tape to secure the towel with some strong tape so that it does not trip your child. Fine Motor Play Pipe cleaners -plastic strainer
Thursday	Letter of the Week: Bb Number of the Week :2 Color of the Week: Blue Shape of the Week: Triangle Your choice book!	Body Trace: Use butcher paper or shelf paper (Should be the length of your child's body). Have your child lie down on the floor. Use a washable marker or crayon to trace them. Have them draw on their eyes,	Sensory Bin Fill your bin with the following: -dry beans -plastic bowls -plastic soup spoons Always supervise when child uses small items!	Zig Zag Run! Place painter's tape on the floor in a zig zag so that it forms a line across the room pattern. Have your child run through the zig zag pattern.	Lego Block Home! You're your child build their Lego home! Questions to ask: Where do you live? What color is your house? Who lives in your house?	Body Trace: - butcher paper/white shelf paper. -washable markers/crayons Sensory Bin: -plastic container big enough to fit 3 pairs of shoes -dry beans -big plastic soup spoons

		nose, and a smile! Ask them how many feet they have? How many hands they have? How many ears they have? How many fingers?				-plastic bowls Note: Always supervise your child when playing with small objects that may pose choking hazard! Zig Zag Run -painter's tape If you are doing the zig zag challenge outside chalk will work great! Build a Lego House! -Lego blocks
Friday	Letter of the Week: Bb Number of the Week :2 Color of the Week: Blue	Paint the Letter B Blue Using a black marker and white construction paper draw	Sensory Squish Bag Grab a Ziploc Bag Fill it with Shaving Cream and add a drop of washable	Line Jump Place some painter's tape on the floor to form separate horizontal	Connect the Numbers! Fold a white print paper in half (vertical wise) Using a black	Letter B Craft: -blue Washable paint -white construction paper

	Shape of the Week: Triangle

Your choice book! | a large letter "B". The letter should take up most of the page!

Give your child some washable blue paint and a paint brush!

Have them trace the letter!

Have them dip their finger in some washable blue paint and dot around the letter!

-As you are working on the craft ask them to think of things that are also blue! | blue, red, and yellow paint as well.

Make sure you seal the bag up tight.

Tape the bag down to the table and have your child squish the bag for some non-messy painting! | lines (10 lines)!

Space the lines far enough to give your child room to jump from line to line as you count the jumps out loud.

If you prefer to do this activity outside you can use side walk chalk to draw lines. | marker/pen write down the following:

1
2
1
2

Give your child a blue crayon and have them draw a line from one side to the matching number on the other side. | -black marker

Sensory Squish Bag:

-Large Ziploc bag

-Shaving Cream

-washable paint: blue is a must since it is the color of the week, but the other two colors can be switched out with colors of your choice!

Line Jump:

-painter's tape

If you are working outdoors you can also use sidewalk chalk

Connect the Numbers

-black pen/marker |

						-printer paper -blue crayon

All About Me Theme Unit: Week 3

	Circle Time	Craft	Sensory	Gross Motor	Fine Motor	Materials Needed
Monday	Letter of the Week: Cc Number of the Week :3 Color of the Week: Green Shape of the Week: Square Book of Your Choice!	C is for Cat Pre-Cut a Large Letter C using white construction paper. The letter should be about half the size of the original paper. -cut out 2 smaller triangles for cat ears -cut out a small pink triangle (the nose) Also have googly eyes, and fuzzy pom poms on hand. Have your child glue the ears to the letter C and glue the fuzzy pom poms on the C to make it	Sensory Squish Bag: Draw a happy monster face using permanent marker. (A Circle and a zig zag smile will work just fine!) Fill a Ziploc bag with clear hair gel Add a Few googly eyes to the mix! Seal and tape the bag to the table. Have your child have fun moving googly eyes around the silly monster face!	Shoot Some Hoops! Place a laundry basket on the floor. Give your child a bin full of 10 rolled socks! Count to ten as your child makes some game winning shots!	Square Art Using a black marker, draw a large square on a piece of white construction paper (It should take up most of the page). Using green construction paper cut smaller squares (enough to fill the area of the large square). Have your child glue the smaller squares inside of the big square.	C is For Cat Craft: - white and pink construction paper -fuzzy pom poms -googly Eyes Sensory Squish Bag: Large Ziploc Bag -clear hair gel -googly Eyes -tape -marker Shoot Some Hoops Activity: -clean rolled up socks (1) -laundry basket Square Art

		look like a fuzzy cat. Have them glue on the two googly eyes, and the pink triangle nose! As you are working on the craft ask the child what their favorite animal is.				-white construction paper -glue -green construction paper -scissors -black marker
Tuesday	Letter of the Week: Cc Number of the Week :3 Color of the Week: Green Shape of the Week: Square Book of Your Choice!	Decorate the Number 3! Draw a Large number 3 on piece of blue construction paper. (It should take up most of the page). Give your child a paint brush and some washable green paint. Have them trace the number 3. When the paint dries	Sensory Bin: Fill the bin with multicolor Lego blocks! Have your child identify the green Legos!	Duck Waddle Blow up two balloons! One your child and one for a friend! Have them place balloon between legs and waddle to the finish line! If a buddy their age is not available feel free to join in the fun!	Yarn Hair Cut! Grab a few strands of yarn. Tie them together and one end so that the strings hang loose on the other end like a pony tail. Have your child use scissors to cut pretend hair! As they are working ask them:	Decorate the Number 3! -Green washable paint -dry beans -blue construction paper -glue Sensory Bin: -plastic bin large enough to fit 3 pairs of shoes! -multicolor Lego blocks!

		have them glue dry beans along the lines of the number. supervise child whenever they are working with small items)			What color is your hair? Is your hair curly or straight? Make sure to complement their beautiful hair!	Duck Waddle: -balloons Yarn Hair Cut: -yarn -rubber band or hair tie -child friendly scissors Always supervise your child when working with scissors!
Wednesday	Letter of the Week: Cc Number of the Week :3 Color of the Week: Green Shape of the Week: Square Book of Your Choice!	Fingerprint Leaves!! Using washable brown paint and a paint brush draw a tree trunk on a piece of white construction paper. Dip your child's fingers into	Mr. Potato Head feature search: Fill your chosen sensory bag with un pop corn kernels! Throw in separated feature pieces of	Bean Bag Shape Toss! Draw a square, triangle, and circle on different sheets of print paper. Make them large enough for your child to see from a distance!	Fuzzy Pom Pom Drop! Tape empty paper towel or toilet paper rolls on your wall. Have your child drop different color pom poms down each roll. As they drop the pom	Fingerprint Tree: -green and brown washable paint -paint brush -white construction paper Sensory Bin: Mr. Potato Head

		some washable green finger-paint paint! Have them use their fingerprints to create the green leaves on the branches of the tree. Questions to ask your child: -What color is the paint on your fingers? How many fingers do you have? Count their fingers with them!	Mr. Potato Head! Have your child find and identify the different features! Note: Always supervise your child when using any small item.)	Tape each paper to the floor. Give your child a bucket of bean bags! Have the child identify each shape before they toss the bean bag to the correct shape!	poms, have them identify the color of the pom.	feature search: -plastic bin large enough to fit 3 pairs of shoes Mr. Potato Head features: eyes, nose, mouth, ears, etc. (If one is not available you can draw facial features on a piece of paper or you can cut out facial features from a magazine. -un-popped popcorn corn kernels ALWAYS supervise your child when playing with small objects that may pose choking hazard! Bean Bag Shape Toss:

						-Paper with designated shapes printed on them large enough from the middle of the room.

-Bean Bags (If non available rolled socks will work as substitute.

-tape

-plastic bucket |
| Thursday | Letter of the Week: Cc

Number of the Week:3

Color of the

Week: Green

Shape of the Week: Square

Book of Your Choice! | Foot Print Buddy!

Using washable paint have your child create their foot prints on a piece of white construction paper. (Have the child choose either the color of the week or a color from the previous weeks to review | Sensory Balloons.

Use a funnel to fill balloons with different items

Fill the first balloon with beans

-the second one with flour

The third with water (just enough to make it squishy!) Have the | Ball Transfer

Fill a basket with balloons

. Take a second empty basket and place it next to the filled basket.

Have your child sit on a chair and transfer the balls from one basket to another | Pom Pom water bottle push!

Count out loud with your child as they fill a water bottle with fuzzy multicolor pom poms! | Foot Print Buddy!

-white construction paper

Washable Green, Blue, or yellow paint

-googly eyes

-glue

-washable marker for drawing smile

Sensory Balloons |

		acquired knowledge. Once the paint dries have your child glue on googly eyes to their footprints and use a washable marker to draw on smile!	child feel and describe the different textures.	using their feet!		-balloons -flour -dry beans -water (just a little not too much to avoid popping!) Ball Transfer: Two Empty Baskets or Bins Big enough to fit at least 5 inflated balloons -Balloons
Friday	Letter of the Week: Cc Number of the Week :3 Color of the Week: Green Shape of the Week: Square Book of Your Choice!	Name Craft Using a black marker, write down your child's first name on a piece green construction paper. It should take up at least half of the paper! Help them trace the lines of the letters of	Shaving Cream Fun! Place a plastic mat on your table. Add two hands full of shaving cream. Have your child practice writing the letter C, the number 3, and drawing squares with their fingers!	ABC Broom Hockey! Write Down the Letter "C" on two paper plates and then tape them together! Have your child use a broom to sweep the plate into the goal! Set up a chair for the goal post!	Alphabet Pancakes! Cut up medium sized circles using a cardboard box. Using a black marker write down the letter's "A", "B", "C" on the circles. Have your child use a spatula to flip over the pretend	Name Craft: - Constructio n paper -glue -black marker - Cheerios! (Review the ingredients on the box to make sure your baby isn't allergic to any of the ingredients.

		their name with glue! Have them cover the lines with cheerios! As they are working on their project make sure to complement their name and tell them what an amazing job they are doing!	Feel free to join them in the messy fun!	Set it up across the room from the starting point!	pancakes! As they are working review the letters with them!	Sensory Fun: -Shaving Cream -ABC Hockey: -2 paper plates -tape -marker -Broom (make sure to clean the chosen broom before you begin. If possible, use a child size toy broom. -Chair Alphabet Pancakes! -Cardboard -plastic spatula -scissors -black marker

All About Me Theme Unit: Week: 4

	Circle Time	Craft	Sensory	Gross Motor	Fine Motor	Materials
Monday	Letter of the Week: Dd Number of the Week :4 Color of the Week: Orange Shape of the Week : Diamond Your choice book!	D is for Donut! Fold a paper plate in half. Cut the letter D in the middle of the plate. When you open the plate up it should have whole in the middle! Give your child washable paint dotters (different colors). Have your child use a washable paint dotters to decorate their donut! Tell them the dots are sprinkles! If a dotter is unavailable you can also use cotton balls to dot with	Sensory Bin Fill your bin with the following: -plastic funnels -dry oatmeal -plastic cups	Colorful Diamonds: On 4 separate sheets of white print paper draw a big diamond shape. One diamond per paper, and make sure to draw each diamond with a different color marker. Colors :blue, green, yellow, red and orange Tape the diamonds to a wall. Make sure that they are tape low enough for your child to reach them. Place an empty cup below	Mystery Color package! Using gift wrapping, paper, wrap the following items: orange crayon/Mar ker -Orange or Tangerine -Carrot -Have your child unwrap the mystery packages! Have them identify each item and their color!	Letter D Craft: -paper plate -washable paint dotters Note: If dotters are not available use cotton balls and washable paint instead! Sensory Bin: -plastic container large enough to fit 3 pairs of shoes -plastic funnels (If you do not have any funnels you can also make a funnel out of a rolled up piece of construction paper and tape!)

		washable paint!		the wall of diamonds! Across the room, place a cup of red, blue, yellow, and orange colored crayons next to your child. Tell them to choose a color crayon. Have your child hop, tippy toe, or lunge across the room until they reach the wall of diamonds. Tell them make a mark with their crayon on matching color diamond! Then have them place their crayon in the empty cup. Once they are done they can walk, run,		-plastic cups Mystery Color Package: -Any gift wrapping paper will do! -Tape -Tangerine/Orange -Carrot -Orange Crayon or marker

				hop, or tippy toe back to their starting point. -repeat until all of the crayons are inside the original empty cup!		
Tuesday	Letter of the Week: Dd Number of the Week: 4 Color of the Week: Orange Shape of the Week: Diamond Your Choice Book!	What's behind the door? Fold a piece of construction paper in half. On the front flap of the paper draw a door handle. On the inside of the paper draw a large number 4. Tell your child that the front flap of the paper is a door. Have them decorate the door with their choice of décor:	Sensory Bin: Fill your bin with the following: -dry rice, and plastic scoops Make sure to place a mat underneath your sensory play area. Rice can get messy.	Color ball sort! Place your multicolor plastic balls in basket/or bucket. (The kind of plastic balls you find inside ball pit!) Place 3 different containers with different color construction paper taped to their side (choose two of the previous week's colors, and the color orange).	Snack Bracelet! Have your child thread cheerios or fruit loops using pipe cleaners! Make sure to supervise them. When they are done threating twists the ends together to form a bracelet. Make sure the pointy side of the pipe cleaner is tucked in nicely. You do not want accidental snack bracelet scratches!	What's behind the door? -construction paper(any color -your choice of decorations (feathers, glitter, buttons, etc.) -marker to draw number -glue Sensory Bin: -plastic bin large enough to fit 3 pairs of shoes -dry rice

		buttons, feathers, glitter, etc. As they are working on their door craft have them count the corners 1,2,3,4. Once they are done chant with them 1,2,3,4, let's find out what's behind the door. When you open the flap say enthusiastically "It's the number 4!"		Place the 3 containers across the room from the container holding all of the multicolor balls. Have your child use a big plastic soup spoon or ladle to carry the different balls across the room and drop them in the correct color box. (If multicolor ball pit balls are not available feel free to use multicolor rolled up socks!		-Different sized plastic funnels (remember you can make funnels by rolling up a piece of paper, and securing it with a piece of scotch tape. -plastic cups Color Ball Sort: -plastic ball pit balls 4 different containers -multi color construction paper that match the color of the plastic balls being used. Note: At least one of the papers should be orange. -Tape
Wednesday	Letter of the Week: Dd Number of the Week: 4	Carrot Sponge Paint!	Sensory Bin:	Soccer with Mom! Have your child	Shapes and fuzzy pom-poms!	Carrot Sponge Paint:

	Color of the Week: Orange Shape of the Week: Diamond Your Choice Book!	Using a black marker, draw a carrot shape on a piece of construction paper! It should take up at least half of the size of the paper. -Use a piece of one of your kitchen sponges to have your child sponge paint the orange carrot!	Fill your bin with the following: -black beans -plastic mini shovels -carrots (You can use real or plastic toy carrots).	practice kicking a ball with you! If possible, enjoy this activity outdoor! However, if you are unable to venture out feel free to clear a space in your chosen room for some soccer fun! If a soccer ball is unavailable you can always stuff a pillow case with socks dish towels. Fill it so it's nice and firm for a good kick!	Secure shelf paper on the wall. Have the sticky side facing the child. Draw a three large shapes on the paper. Diamond, Circle, and Triangle. Have the child take turns identifying each shape. Have them place fuzzy pom- poms on the shape as they identify the correct one.	-black marker -Orange washable paint -Sponge -Construction paper (any color). Sensory Bin: -Plastic container big enough to fit 3 pairs of shoes -black beans -plastic shovels note: child sand castles shovels work best, but you could substitute with plastic soup spoons or cups. -Carrots (real or plastic).
Thursday	Letter of the Week: Dd	Diamond Turtle! Cut out 5 small	Duck Pond! Fill up your chosen sensory bin	Ring Toss: Cut out the middle of 3 paper plates	Build towers with Legos!	Materials Needed:

	Number of the Week :4 Color of the Week: Orange Shape of the Week: Diamond Your Choice Book!	diamond shapes using your color choice or construction paper! Cut out one large diamond as well. The large diamond will be the turtle shell! The small diamonds will be used for the head, and the 4 flippers. Help your child assembled the diamond turtle using glue. Questions to ask as they are working? What shape is this? -What color is this? How many diamonds do you see?	with water. Toss in a few fuzzy pom- poms! Give your child a straw. Have them blow air through the straw in order to move the ducks from one side to the other!	in order to form rings. Color two of the rings with previous' weeks' colors, but make sure that at least one of the rings is orange. (For this activity you can either quick color the rings yourself or you can extend the fun by having your child help you do it!) Tape a paper towel roll down to a plate so that it stands up vertically (This is your ring pole). Have your child practice tossing their hitting their mark with	Questions to ask: -what colors can you see? -How many Lego's are in the tower? -What's your favorite color?	Diamond Turtle Craft: -Constructio n paper (your color choice!) -scissors -glue Duck Pond: Sensory Bin: -plastic bin large enough to fit 3 pairs of shoes -water -straws - fuzzy pom-poms Colorful Ring Toss! -Paper Plates -Your Choice of: crayons/mar kers, colored pencils -empty paper -empty paper towel Roll

		-Have them practice counting with you.		their colored rings!		-tape -scissors Lego Towers -multicolor Lego blocks
Friday	Letter of the Week: Dd Number of the Week 4 Color of the Week: Orange Shape of the Week: Diamond Your Choice Book!	Shape Face Using your choice color of construction paper cut out the following shapes: two circles for the eyes a triangle for the nose a diamond mouth Cut two squares for the ears Using a paper plate as a base help your child build their shape face. As your child is building their shape face ask the	No Mess Shaving Cream Letters: Fill up a large Ziploc bag with shaving cream. Seal the bag and tape it down to the table. Have your child practice writing Letters "Aa" through "Dd" with their fingers	Alphabet Catch! Sing the letters of the alphabet as you play a game of catch!	Bingo! Fold a sheet of regular print paper so that when you unfold the paper it contains 6 squares. In 2 of the squares write down the letter Dd. -Color in another square with the color orange -Fill in another square with the number 4 -in another draw a diamond shape	Materials needed: Shape Face: Construction paper cut outs: -two circles -one triangle -one diamond -two squares -paper plate No Mess Shaving Cream: -Ziploc bag -shaving cream -tape Alphabet Catch: Child Friendly Bouncy Ball!

| | | following questions:

-What shape is this?

-What color is this?

-How many circles are there?

-How many squares? | | | -in the last square draw triangle.

-Have your child identify the contents of each box.

Give them a plastic cup of cheerios or goldfish snack crackers. As they identify each box have them place a snack in the box. | Snack Bingo!

-sheet of paper divided into 6 squares

-Goldfish or cheerios |

Theme: Fall   Week: 1

	Circle Time	Craft	Sensory	Gross Motor	Fine Motor	Materials Needed
Monday	Letter of the Week: Ee Number of the Week:5 Color of the Week: Brown Shape of the Week: Rectangle Your Choice Book!	E is for Elephant! Paint the inside of your child's hand grey, then have them place their hand on a piece of white construction paper. The thumb is the trunk, and the other 4 fingers are the legs of the elephant Once the paint dries have your child add 2 googly eyes to the hand print. Use a washable black marker to draw on a happy smile on it, and some elephant ears!	Sensory Bin: Pumpkin Wash! Add the following to your sensory bin: -water -5 hand sized pumpkins -bath bubbles -dish brush.	Spider Web Obstacle Course! Using painters tape create a spider web on the floor! Have your child pretend that they are a spider crawling through their web! -	Tree Art Using brown washable paint and a paint brush, paint the trunk and branches of a tree on a white construction paper. Now give the paper to your child, Give them washable red, orange, brown, and yellow paint Have them dip Q-tips into the paints and dot Fall leaves on the tree.	E is for Elephant Craft: -white construction paper -grey washable paint! -googly eyes -washable black marker to draw on ear and happy smile -glue Sensory Bin: -plastic bin large enough to fit 3 pairs of shoes 5 small hand sized pumpkins -water -bubble bath soap -dish brush (soft bristle) Note: Always Supervise

						your child when playing with a tub of water! Tree Art -Q-Tips -red, orange, yellow, and brown washable paint -white construction paper -paint brush
Tuesday	Letter of the Week: Ee Number of the Week :5 Color of the Week: Brown Shape of the Week: Rectangle Book of Your Choice!	5 Little Pumpkins! Directions: Cut an apple in half. Have your child dip the flat side of the apple in some washable orange paint. Then have them stamp the apple 5 times onto a black piece of construction paper. Make sure to count the pumpkins with your child.	Sensory Play: Cut the top off a medium sized pumpkin. Scoop the pumpkin guts out and place them on a plastic mat or plastic container. Have your child squish them with their hands. -Ask them how do	Monster Bowling. Use water bottles as pins. Using a marker draw silly monster faces on them! Set the pins up for your child and have them use a child sized ball to knock the pins down!	Spin the Web! Have your child pull apart cotton balls and glue them onto a black piece of construction paper to create a spider's web!	5 Little Pumpkins Craft: ½ of an Apple -orange washable paint -black construction paper Pumpkin Wash: Sensory Play: -medium Sized Pumpkin -plastic mat

		Questions to ask: What color is it? How many pumpkins do you see?	they feel on your skin? -What color are they? Note: Make sure to supervise your child whenever they are working with small objects such as seeds. Small items may pose choking hazard.			-pumpkin cutter (will help you to remove pumpkin top to retrieve the guts). You do the cutting of the top yourself. Safety First! Note: Always supervise your child when playing with small objects that my pose choking hazards! - Monster Bowling: 5-10 Water Bottles. (Empty is fine but if you are outside and it is windy you might want to used filled ones. -Child sized bouncy ball! Spin the Web: -Cotton Balls

						-Glue -Black Construction Paper
Wednesday	Letter of the Week: Ee Number of the Week: 5 Color of the Week: Brown Shape of the Week: Rectangle Your Choice of Book!	Bear Craft: -Precut 2 hand sized circles using brown construction paper. These are the bear's ears. -Precut 1 palm sized triangle using black construction paper. This is the bear's nose! Directions: Give your child a paper plate. Have them dip their plastic fork in washable brown paint then stamp it down all over the paper plate. It will look like they are	Sensory Bin Fill your bin with the following: -small apples -dry Oatmeal -plastic funnels	Stop and Go! Play a game of stop and go using your child's favorite fast beat song! When the music starts to play have them perform a specific exercise ex) running in place, jumping jacks, lunges etc. As soon as they hear the music have, they are to start the task, but as soon as the music stops they must stop as well. Alternate between your chosen exercises.	Pasta Strings! Use play dough as a base. Place 5 strands of individual pasta so that they stand up vertically! Have your child string cheerios on each strand. As they are stringing their cheerios have them count each ring!	Bear Craft: -paper Plate -brown construction -black construction paper -googly eyes -brown washable paint -plastic fork -Sensory Bin: -plastic container large enough to fit 3 pairs of shoes -dry oatmeal -5 small apples -plastic funnels Stop and Go -Your Child's favorite fast beat song

		painting brown fur! When they are done and the paint has dried have your child glue the two brown circles to the plate. These are the two bear ears. Have them glue the triangle nose and two googly eyes Enjoy your brown bear craft!		Feel Free to Join in the Fun! Safety First: Make sure your child is comfortable doing your chosen movements, and that they are hydrated. If your child becomes tired do not force them to keep going. Take breaks as needed and always modify when necessary! This should be a fun energy burner!		-water Safety First! Make sure your child is both comfortable performing your chosen exercises. Make sure they are hydrated. Pasta Strings! -play dough -dry Pasta Linguini -Cheerios
Thursday	Letter of the Week: Ee Number of the Week :5 Color of the	Rectangle googly eyed Monster! Have your child tear small pieces of green tissue paper.	Sensory Bin Fill your bin with the following:	Rake the Fall Leaves! Using painters tape create the following shapes on the floor: rectangle,	Play Dough Fun! Draw a large number 5 on a regular sheet of paper. It should take up at least	Rectangle Googly eyed Monster! -googly eyes -green tissue paper

	Week: Brown Shape of the Week: Rectangle Your Choice Book!	-Present them with a pre-drawn large rectangle on a sheet of construction paper. Have them cover the rectangle completely with their torn tissue paper. When they are done have them add 3 googly eyes!	-cotton balls -plastic spiders -child friendly tweezers.	triangle, and a square. Place dry leaves on the Floor. Feel free to use pretend leaves if real leaves are not available! -Have your child take turns raking the leaves into each of the shapes! (A clean broom will serve as a rake).	half of the paper. Have the child use play dough to trace the lines of the number 5	-construction paper (your choice color). -washable black marker to draw shape! Sensory Bin: -plastic bin large enough to fit 3 pairs of shoes -cotton balls -child friendly tweezers -plastic spiders Rake the Fall Leaves Activity: -painter's tape Fall Leaves: (Real or Decorative if none are available you can always make some out of tissue paper. -broom (child sized).

						Play Dough Fun! -regular sheet of paper (line or print). -play dough -pen or marker to draw number 5
Friday	Letter of the Week: Ee Number of the Week: 5 Color of the Week: Brown Shape of the Week: Rectangle Your Choice Book!	Fall Leaf Craft! Using cardboard paper, cut out a big fall leaf shape at least as big as half the size of a sheet of paper. Place the cut out on top of a black piece of construction paper. Hold the shape down as your child colors over it using Yellow, Orange, and Brown Chalk! Make sure that they	Sensory Bag! Fill a large Ziploc bag with hair gel and some glitter! Make sure the bag is super sealed and secured to a table with tape. Have your child practice drawing shapes on it for some non-messy fun!	Letter E Hunt! Using a washable marker. write down the Letter "Ee" on different Legos -Hide them around the house or outside! Give your child a basket or bag. Have them go on a Letter "Ee" hunt!	Number Bend! Help your child use pipe cleaners to form the Numbers 1 through 5	Fall Leaf Craft -Chalk: brown, orange, and yellow -Black Construction paper -cardboard Glitter Squish Bag -large Ziploc Bag -hair gel -glitter -tape Note: When working with glitter always Make sure the bag is super-

		cover the entire area around the leaf! When you lift up the shape the leaf print should remain!				duper sealed before giving it to your child! Letter "Ee" Lego Hunt! -dry erase washable markers -Legos -basket (to collect Lego blocks!) Number Bend: Child Friendly Pipe Cleaners (Always Watch out for any pointy ends!)

Theme: Fall Week: 2

	Circle Time	Craft	Sensory	Gross Motor	Fine Motor	Materials Needed
Monday	Letter of the Week: Ff Number of the Week: 6 Color of the Week: Black Shape of the Week: Oval Your Choice Book!	F is for Fish Craft: Cut a Half a page sized triangle out of a piece of orange construction paper! (The Triangle will be used for the Tail.) Dip your child's fingers in orange washable finger paint! Have them leave their multiple prints on a paper plate. Tell them that these are the fish scales! When the paint has tried have them glue two googly eyes on the fish and draw a smile! Help them to glue on the triangle fish tail to the side of the	Sensory Bin: Pasta Play! Fill your chosen plastic sensory bin with the following: -dry elbow pasta and plastic scoops!	Acorn Race! Give your child a spoon and a plastic bowl full of acorns. Using regular print/lined paper and different colored markers draw 4 ovals. One oval per sheet. Each oval should be a different color. Next tape each shape to 4 different plastic bins. Stand next to the 4 bins with the ovals taped on them. Have power walk towards you with the acorn in their spoon. When they get to the bins have	Salt Tray Have your child practice Drawing Letters A-F on the Salt Tray	F is for Fish Craft: -paper plate -washable orange finger paint -orange construction paper half a page triangle for tail. -googly eyes Sensory Bin: -plastic container big enough to fit 3 pairs of shoes -dry pasta Scoops Acorn Race: -acorns Note: If none are available you can substitute with cotton balls, or baby socks socks) -4 plastic bins

		plate!(Only one corner of the triangle should be touching the plate).		them identify the color of the oval before dropping in their acorn! Have them walk back and repeat until all the acorns are in the bins!		-4 different colored markers (make sure at least one of the markers is the color of the week.) -print/lined paper -tape Salt Tray: -child's tray table deep enough so that salt will not spill over. Note: You can also substitute tray with a paper plate. Make sure to place a plastic mat beneath the salt to avoid messy clean up!
Tuesday	Letter of the Week: Ff Number of the Week: 6 Color of the	Oval Bat and hand prints Cut out an oval shape the size of your hand using a black construction paper.	Sensory Bin: Fill your bin with the following: -dry black beans and glow in the	Monster Tumble: Draw silly faces on 6 cups! Have your child count them! Set up the cups so your child can	Pumpkin Thumbtack geo board Parents: Push multiple thumbtacks into a medium sized	Oval Bat Craft: -black construction paper -yellow construction paper

	Week: Black Shape of the Week: Oval Your Choice Book!	Have your child glue the Oval onto a yellow construction paper. -Use a soft brush to paint the inside of your child's hands with a washable kid friendly nontoxic paint. Have them press their hands on either side of the oval to create bat wings! When your child is done have them glue on some fun googly eyes!	dark mini Stars Note: Always supervise your child when they are working with small objects that may pose choking hazard!	knock them down with a small ball or a rolled-up sock!	pumpkin! Make sure they are pushed all the way in and are secure! Help your child create multiple shapes using rubber bands on the pumpkin geoboard.	-glue -googly eyes -washable nontoxic kid friendly washable black paint -Sensory Bin: -plastic container that can fit at least 3 pairs of shoes! -black beans -glow in the dark stars Note: Always supervise your child when working with small objects that may pose choking hazard. Monster Tumble: -plastic Cups -marker: to draw silly monster faces! -Small child sized and child friendly

						ball/ rolled up socks! Pumpkin Geoboard! -thumbtacks (Parents make sure you push them all the way in. And supervise your child while they are working on this activity.) -rubber bands -medium sized pumpkin (Always supervise your child when working with small objects that may pose choking hazard.)
Wednesday	Letter of the Week: Ff Number of the Week :6	Silver Moon Craft Draw a large circle on a black piece of construction paper using white chalk. It	Sensory Bin: Cooked spaghetti! Tell your child the noodles are	ABC Leaf Hop! Write down letters A-F on different sheets of paper. Cut the paper so that	Play Dough and Scissors! Have your child practice cutting with some child	Silver moon Craft: -black construction paper -silver or white

	Color of the Week: Black Shape of the Week: Oval Your Choice Book!	should take up most of the paper. Have your child use a clothespin to dip cotton balls into silver or white paint. Then have your child dot the inside of the circle until it is covered with paint.	pretend wiggly worms!	they take the shape of leaves (think oval shape.) Tape them securely to the floor. Have your child hop from letter to letter! If you are outdoors use sidewalk chalk to write the letters!	friendly scissors and some squishy play dough.	washable paint -clothespin -cotton balls Sensory Bin: -plastic container that large enough to fit 3 pairs of shoes! -cooked spaghetti ABC Leaf Hop! -Marker -regular print paper will work, but it is more fun if you use a variety of colors. -tape (note if you are completing this activity outdoors you can simply use sidewalk chalk to write down the letters!) Play Dough and scissors! -play dough

						-child Friendly Scissors
Thursday	Letter of the Week: Ff

Number of the Week :6

Color of the

Week: Black

Shape of the Week: Oval

Your Choice Book! | Pumpkin Patch

On a piece of yellow construction paper, draw a large letter "Ff" using green paint.

Have your child dip their fingers into some washable orange paint.

Next have your child leave multiple finger prints along the lines of the Letter "Ff". | Fall Leaf Sensory Bin

Fill your sensory bin with some beautiful fall leaves.

Questions to ask:

How do they feel?

What color is it? | Play a game of Simon Says using a small pumpkin!

Example: Simon Says jump over the pumpkin

Simon Says march around the room with the pumpkin on your head! | On a regular sheet of paper draw an oval, a triangle, and a square using broken lines --------

Have your child use a black crayon to trace each shape. | Pumpkin Patch:

-yellow construction paper

-green washable paint

-paint brush

-orange washable finger-paint

Fall Leaf Sensory Bin

-Any plastic container large enough to fit 3 pairs of shoes!

-Fall Leaves Note: if you do not have leaves available a mixture of orange, red, and yellow bits of tissue paper will work just fine! |

| Friday | Letter of the Week: Ff

Number of the Week :6

Color of the Week: Black

Shape of the Week: Oval

Your Choice Book! | Monster Teeth!

Use green construction paper to cut out an oval shape! The oval should take up most of the page!

Draw a horizontal line across the middle.

Have your child glue 6 pieces of candy corn on the line. Tell them they are monster teeth! | Sensory Bin

Fill your chosen bin with the following:

-candy corn

-plastic measuring cups

Questions to ask:
How do they smell!

What shape is it?

What colors do you see?

Always Supervise your child when playing with small items! | Catch the Bat!

Using black construction paper cut out 6 triangles about the size of your hand!

Blow up 3 green balloons.

Tape 2 triangles to the sides of each balloon (these are your bat wings!)

Draw two eyes and a zig zag smiles on each bat!

Toss the Balloons in the air!

Have your child run to catch them while they are in flight!

Repeat multiple times for some bat fun! | Unwrap the Mummy!

Have your child

Wrap a hand sized pumpkin with multiple rubber bands. Tell your child to unwrap the mummy! | Monster Teeth:

-green construction paper

-candy corn!

-glue

-marker

Candy Corn Sensory Bin:

-plastic container that large enough to fit 3 pairs of shoes!

-candy corn (Always supervise your child when working with small items that may pose choking hazard).

-plastic measuring cups

Catch the Bat:

-3 Green Balloons

-black construction paper |
|---|---|---|---|---|---|

						-black marker
						-tape
						Unwrap the Mummy:
						Hand sized pumpkins
						-rubber bands

Theme: Fall Week: 3

	Circle time	Craft	Sensory	Gross Motor	Fine Motor	Materials Needed
Monday	Letter of the Week: Gg Number of the Week :7 Color of the Week: Purple Shape of the Week: Pentagon Your Choice Book!	Letter "Gg" Craft Draw the Letter G on a yellow construction paper. Have your child use purple dotter to trace the letter "Gg". Tell them that "Gg" is for grapes!	Sensory Bin Mix some water and purple food coloring together. Place the colored water in ice 2-3 ice trays and freeze them. Drop the purple ice cubes in the sensory bin. Give your child two smaller plastic containers. Have your child take turns transferring the frozen purple pops to different containers using the plastic soup spoons!	Apple Sauce! Fill up 7 small red or green water balloons! Write and place the number 7 in different locations in an outside area. Have your child take aim with their balloon from a distance. When the balloon hits the target yell out Apple Sauce! -If you have concrete outdoor area use sidewalk chalk to write down the number 7 in various places.	Pumpkin Bag! Have your child tear orange tissue paper into small pieces, have them fill a zip lock bag with the orange pieces. Once they are done. Draw two triangle eyes and triangle nose and a happy smile!	Letter "Gg" Craft -yellow construction paper -purple dotter -marker to draw letter Sensory Bin: -plastic container that can fit 3 pairs of shoes! -purple food coloring 2-3 ice cube trays -water -2 plastic bowls - 2 plastic soup spoons Apple Sauce Activity Indoors:

58

				-If you have a grass yard write the number down on a regular sheet of paper and place them around your yard. -If you are doing this activity indoors use a sheet of paper to write down the number 7 multiple times and then tape them to different areas. Have your child use rolled up socks to hit the target instead of water balloons!		Regular sheets of paper -tape -rolled socks -marker Outdoors with concrete: -red or green water balloons -side walk Chalk Outdoors on grass: -paper -tape -water balloons -Marker
Tuesday	Letter of the Week: Gg Number of the Week 7 Color of the Week: Purple	Pentagon Craft Using Purple construction paper draw a large pentagon (it should take	Sensory Bin Fill your bin with the following: -rocks -sticks -leaves	Owl Eyes! Using 7 sticky notes write down the letter "Gg". Place the sticky notes in your	Pumpkin Lacing Use a hole puncher to make multiple holes through out	Pentagon Craft: -purple construction paper -cotton balls -glue

| | Shape of the Week : Pentagon

Your Choice Book! | up most of the paper).

-Have your child pull apart cotton balls and then glue the pieces along the lines of the pentagon. Tell them the pentagon is the shape of house! This house has a family of silly spiders and these are their webs! | Questions to ask:

What is it?

How does it feel? | chosen darkened room.

Give your child a flashlight. Together walk around the darkened room. Use your own flashlight your owl eyes to search for the letter "Gg"! Have fun!

Safety First:

Make sure to remove any tripping hazards before darkening the room. Do not make it pitch black. Make sure to stay next to your child as you search the room together. You should have your own | a paper plate.

Give your child orange yarn to lace their pumpkin. | Sensory Bin:

Dry Leaves

Sticks and Rocks (Always supervise your child when they are playing with small objects that may pose a choking hazard).

Owl Eyes:

-sticky notes:

-marker/pen

-flashlight

Pumpkin Lacing:

-paper plate

-orange yarn

-hole puncher |

				flashlight too!		
Wednesday	Letter of the Week: Gg Number of the Week 7 Color of the Week: Purple Shape of the Week: Pentagon Your Choice Book!	Fall Leaves Cut 10 squares from either yellow, or orange tissue paper. Cut 2 hand sized oval shapes from a piece of black construction paper. Have your child glue and place all of the tissue paper pieces onto the black piece of construction paper. Make sure to help them spread out the pieces so that the leaf is fully covered.	Purple Pasta painting! Mixed cooked noodles with washable purple paint. Place the purple noodles on a large piece of construction paper. Have your child play and paint with the noodles for some messy fun!	Pillow Obstacle Course Challenge! Set up an obstacle course for your child using pillows and a balloon! Place the pillows in a way so that your child can crawl, walk, or hop over them (Remember each child is different so make sure that you plan according to your child's personal ability). Safety First!	1-7 Purple Art Write Numbers 1-7 on a sheet of white construction paper. Make them large enough for your child to be able to trace them. Have your child trace the numbers using washable purple paint and Q tips.	Fall Leaves craft: -black piece of construction paper -Your choice of orange, red, or yellow tissue paper -glue Purple Pasta Painting -cooked spaghetti -purple washable paint -large piece of construction paper Also I recommend you place a mat underneath the work station. This activity usually gets pretty messy!

					1-7 Purple Art! -white construction paper -marker to write down numbers -purple washable paint -Q-Tips
Thursday	Letter of the Week: Gg Number of the Week 7 Color of the Week: Purple Shape of the Week: Pentagon Your Choice Book!	Fall Leaf Stamps Have your child paint some Fall leaves using washable paint and their choice of colors. Once the leaves are painted have your child stamp them onto a piece of construction paper. Any color will do. When they lift the leaves up, the shape of the leaf with	Fall Squish Bags! -Fill a Ziploc bag with shaving cream, and some drops of red, yellow, an orange washable paint. Seal the bag and tape it to the table. Have your child mix the Fall Colors together!	Cat Challenge! Using washable child friendly face paint draw some whiskers on your child! Tell them they are a cat! Place 7 cups on the floor in different areas. Hide 4 fuzzy pom poms underneath 4 of the cups. Have your child run from cup to cup trying	Mini Marshmallow Shapes! Using mini Marshmallows and tooth picks. Help your child to build a pentagon, square, and a rectangle.	Fall Leaf Stamp Craft: -large Fall leaves -washable paint (child's choice colors) -construction paper Fall Color Squish Bags: -large Ziploc bag. -Shaving Cream -Washable Paints :red,

| | | their chosen colors should remain. | | to find all the mice until all the pom poms have been collected.

Note: Always supervise your child when working with small objects that may pose choking hazard! | | yellow, and orange

-tape

Cat Challenge:

Washable Face Paint for whiskers

-7 Plastic Cups

4 fuzzy pom poms

Mini Marshmallo w shapes

-mini marshmallo ws

-toothpicks

(Always supervise your child when working with small objects that may pose choking hazard!) |
|---|---|---|---|---|---|---|
| Friday | Letter of the Week: Gg

Number of the Week 7 | Lego Painting (Shape Review)!

On a piece of | Sensory Bottle:

Fill a water bottle with water (a little more | Number Line Run!

Using sidewalk chalk write down | Using a purple construction piece of paper draw the letter | Lego Painting:

-large Legos to make it easy for your child |

Color of the Week: Purple Shape of the Week: Pentagon Your Choice Book!	construction paper draw a pentagon, circle and oval. Place washable paint blobs on a paper plate so your child can dip some Legos into them (Give your child at least 3 choices of color including the color of the week.) Once the child has dipped the Legos into their chosen color have them stamp their Legos onto the pentagon for some color fun!	than half way full). Add 2 drops of baby oil and a drop of purple food coloring. Make sure the lid is tightly shut before you and your child give it a shake!	number 1-7 in a straight line. Make sure the numbers are spread apart! Have your child race through the number line as they are counting from 1-7! If you are doing this activity indoors write the numbers down a pieces of paper and secure them with tape so that your child does not slip!	"Gg" in different areas of the paper at least 10 times. Have your child place stickers on each of the letters. Any sticker will work!	to dip and paint! -black washable marker to draw shapes -Any color construction paper Sensory Bottle: -water bottle with a tight lid -water -baby oil -food coloring (color of the week). Number line race: -sidewalk chalk if completing the activity outdoors -Indoors: -regular print paper with the number written large enough so child can see them as

						they race bye! -tape

Fall Theme Week: 4

	Circle Time	Craft	Sensory	Gross Motor	Fine Motor	Materials Needed
Monday	Letter of the Week: Hh Number of the Week 8 Color of the Week: White Shape of the Week: Trapezoid Book of Choice!	"Hh" is for Hair: Using washable paint have your child paint a paper plate green! -Once the paint has dried give your child some precut strands of yarn to glue onto the sides of the paper plate! This will be hair! Next have your child glue on some googly eyes. Help them to draw on a happy smile!	Sensory Bin Fill your chosen sensory bin with some clean soil, a couple of palm sized pumpkins and some plastic scoops for some Fall fun!	Time's Up! Place some stuffed animals or rolled socks in a basket. Place a second empty basket across the room. Set the timer for (30 seconds). Have your child toss as many stuffed animals or socks as they can into the empty basket before their time runs out! This activity works great outdoors too!	Frozen Googly Eyes! Freeze some googly eyes using water and 2 ice trays! Once they are frozen place them in a plastic bowl. Give your child some kid friendly tweezers to transfer the googly eyes into a second empty container. Have them count out loud as they are making the transfer!	"Hh" is for Hair: -washable green paint -paper plate -any colored yarn -glue Sensory Bin: -clean soil -two palm sized pumpkins - plastic scoops Time's Up Activity: 2 baskets or plastic containers -rolled socks, or stuffed animals -timer Frozen Googly Eyes

						-two ice trays -water -googly eyes -two plastic bowls -child friendly tweezers
Tuesday	Letter of the Week: Hh Number of the Week 8 Color of the Week: White Shape of the Week: Trapezoid Your Choice Book!	Trapezoid Craft: Using a piece of black construction paper draw a trapezoid using white chalk. Note: The shape should take up most of the paper! Dip a couple of pieces of chalk in some water and have your child color their trapezoid using chalk.	Sensory Bin! Fill your bin with some -dry oatmeal -plastic funnels -three to five small apples	Don't wake the cat! Fill a plastic container with 6-10 dry clean yellow sponges. Place the container next to your child. Place second empty container across the room. Tell your child that they are going to pretend that they are a cute little mouse, and that the	Build A Spider Have your child use pipe cleaners to build some cute spiders!	Trapezoid Craft: -black construction paper -multicolor chalk -water Sensory Bin: -plastic bin large enough to fit 3 pairs of shoes -3 to 5 small apples -dry oatmeal -plastic funnels

| | | As they are creating a piece of chalk art have them count the sides of the trapezoid.

Questions to ask:

Which side of the trapezoid is shorter than the others?

How many sides does it have?

How many corners do you see? | | sponges are their pieces of cheese!

They are to take one piece of cheese at a time as fast as they can across the room to their home (the empty bucket) before the cat wakes up (the timer chimes!)

Set the timer for 30 seconds (adjust timer as needed). | | Don't Wake the Cat Activity:

-Clean dry yellow sponges -2 plastic containers timer

Build a Spider:

- Pipe cleaners. |
|---|---|---|---|---|---|---|
| Wednesday | Letter of the Week: Hh

Number of the Week 8

Color of the Week: White

Shape of the Week: Trapezoid | Silly Skeletons!

Paint your child's thumb white using washable paint.

Have them leave their thumb print on a black piece of construction paper. | White Rice Bin:

Sensory Bin:

Add some dry white rice to your sensory bin along with some plastic funnels.

(Always place a mat underneath the working area! This | Number 8 energy burn!

Have your child jump up and down 8 times

Have them touch their toes 8 times

Have them kick their knees up 8 times! | Fuzzy Shapes!

On a piece of construction paper draw a large trapezoid, a triangle, and an oval.

Have your child decorate their shapes with glue | Silly Skeletons:

-white washable paint

-Q- tips

-glue

-washable marker

-black construction paper |

	Your Choice Book!	Help them to glue Q-tips so that they form the body of their silly skeleton You will need 2 Q-tips to form arms 1 Q-tip for Torso 2 Q-tips for legs Once their thumb print has dried draw on two eyes and a smile using a washable marker!	prevents extra clean up time! This is especially true for rice!	Safety First: Always make sure your child is comfortable performing the exercises, and that they are hydrated. Modify tasks as needed.	and fuzzy pom poms!	White Rice Bin: Sensory Bin: -plastic container large enough to fit 3 pairs of shoes! -dry white rice -plastic funnels -plastic mat Fuzzy Shapes: -construction paper (any color). -Fuzzy pom- poms -Glue -washable marker to draw shapes
Thursday	Letter of the Week: Hh Number of the Week 8 Color of the	Candy Corn Hand Print! Paint your child's palm using washable paint. Use	Squish Bag! Draw two triangle eyes and one triangle nose on a	As fast as a scardy cat! Set out 8 child friendly items that are white	Numbers, Letters, and Shapes! Place some sticky shelf	Candy Corn Handprint! -washable paint: white, orange, and yellow

Week: White Shape of the Week: Trapezoid Your Choice Book!	candy corn pattern and colors. - white fingers -yellow upper palm -orange lower palm. Have your child leave their handprint on a black sheet of construction paper.	large Ziploc bag. Fill the bag with shaving cream and orange paint! Seal and tape the bag onto the table. Have your child mix the color and cream for some non-messy pumpkin art!	around the house ex) paper plates, towels, pillows. Place them around the room that you are conducting the activity in. Tell your child they have 1 minute to race around the room and collect all of the items inside a designated container. Set the timer to 1 minute. Ready! Set! Go!	paper on the wall. Secure it with tape. The sticky side should be facing your child. Using a marker draw a trapezoid, the number 8, and the letter H. Have them take turns identifying each one using fall leaves! The sticky side should be able to hold them the full leaf, if not try leaf pieces!	-black construction paper Jack O Lantern Squish Bag -black marker -large Ziploc bag -Shaving cream -tape -orang washable paint As Fast as a Scardy Cat Activity: 8 child friendly white items -large plastic bin -timer Numbers Letters and Shapes Activity: -sticky shelf paper -Fall leaves -marker

Friday	Letter of the Week: Hh Number of the Week 8 Color of the Week: White Shape of the Week : Trapezoid Your Choice Book!	Jack O Lantern Art! Using a piece of black construction paper precut 3 mini triangles they will be used for the eyes and nose of the jack o lantern. Have your child tear pieces of orange tissue paper. Have them glue the collected torn tissue paper onto a water bottle. Have them cover the bottle completely. Once they are done have them glue on two black triangles for the eyes and one black	Sensory Balloons Play! Using a funnel fill 3 balloons up. 1 with beans 1 with flour 1 with a little bit of water. Have your child play with the balloons over a towel or mat. Questions to ask: How does it feel? What do you think is inside? Is it bumpy? Is it squishy?	Trap the Rat! Place black rolled up socks on the floor around the room or outside! Have your child Toss a hula hoop to trap the rat!	Build a Spikey Porcupine! Use a hole puncher to pre poke holes in an empty toilet paper roll! Have your child thread the hole using plastic straws!	Jack O Lantern Art -black construction paper -orange tissue paper -glue -empty water bottle Sensory Balloon Play: 3 Balloons -funnel -dry beans -flour -water Trap the Rat Activity: Black Rolled up Socks 6-8 pairs -Hula hoop Build a porcupine -empty toilet paper roll

		triangle for the nose.				-hole puncher -plastic straws

Thanksgiving Theme Week 1

	Circle Time	Craft	Sensory	Gross Motor	Fine Motor	Materials Needed
Monday	Letter of the Week: Ii

Number of the Week: 9

Color of the Week: Pink

Shape of the Week: Hexagon

Your Choice Book! | I is for Ice Cream!

Precut a triangle using a brown sheet of construction paper (This will be the cone!) It should be about half a page in size.

Have your child glue the cone onto a yellow piece of construction paper.

Place a half a spoon full of shaving cream on top of the cone.

Add a drop of washable pink paint!

Have your child mix the two together using their | Veggie Water Play!

Place some Fall vegetables ex) squash, or pumpkins inside your child's bin.

Add some water and plastic scoops for some veggie water play! | Fun with the number 9!

Write down the number 9 on 4 different paper cups.

Inside each cup place a note:

1Dance, 2Run in place,

3Jump,

4Waddle like turkey!

Mix the cups up.

Have your child choose a cup.

Open the note.

Whatever the note says they have to do for 9 seconds while a fun dance song plays in the background! | Build a hexagon

-On a regular sheet of print or lined paper draw a hexagon.

Help your child use your hexagon drawing as a guide for building their own hexagon out of popsicle sticks. (No need to glue them down just place them together to form the desired shape.) | I is for Ice-cream!

-brown construction paper

-yellow construction paper

-shaving cream

-washable pink paint

-paint brush

Sensory Bin: Veggie Wash

-plastic bin large enough to fit 3 pairs of shoes.

- water Always supervise your child when playing with a water bin.

-Fall veggies (your choice) |

		paint brush for some puffy pink ice cream fun!		Great family activity!		-plastic scoops Fun with the number 9 -4 plastic/paper cups -sticky notes or any piece of paper will work. -your child's favorite dance music -timer Build a popsicle hexagon: -regular sheet of paper -marker -popsicle sticks
Tuesday	Letter of the Week: Ii Number of the Week :9 Color of the Week: Pink	Turkey craft! Precut a circle the size of your palm using brown	Turkey Tambourine! You will need two paper plates.	Dress up like a scarccrow and dance! Give your child a hat	Don't forget the marshmallows! Place some cotton balls in a bowl. Have your	Turkey Craft! -washable brown paint -paper plate

	Shape of the Week: Hexagon

Your Choice Book! | construction paper.

Using washable brown paint have your child paint the inside of a paper plate. This will be your turkey body.

When the paint has dried have them glue on the paper circle to the center of the plate. Next have them glue two googly eyes to the circle.

Next have them glue some store bought colorful feathers to the top of the plate! 9 in total!

Using orange washable paint help your child to paint a turkey beak! | Drop a spoon full of dry beans into a plate.

Place the second plate on top of the plate containing the beans.

Seal the plates together using masking tape!

Have your child decorate the top of the plate with thanksgiving turkey theme stickers! | Short sleeve unbuttoned shirt and some mittens!

Have them dress up and do the scarecrow dance to their favorite song!

Simply call out some silly moves as the song place example:

Wave your hands!

Turn Around

Wiggle your legs like they light as feathers in the wind!

Make sure to demonstrate your silly dance moves! | child take a spoon and scoop them into different plastic/paper cups!

Pretend they are adding marshmallows to some hot chocolate! | -child friendly paint brush

-store bought feathers

-glue

-scissors

-brown construction paper

Turkey tambourine:

-2 paper plates

-dry beans

-masking tape

-Thanksgiving turkey themed stickers

Scare crow dance!

-Hat

-Unbuttoned kids shirt

-mittens

-your child favorite dance song! |

		Make sure they count the feathers as they are working on the project!				
Wednesday	Letter of the Week: Ii Number of the Week: 9 Color of the Week: Pink Shape of the Week: Hexagon Your Choice Book!	Veggie Art! Place a brown sheet of construction paper down in front of your child. Give them an ear of uncooked corn. Place some washable yellow, orange, and red paint drops on the paper. Have your child roll the corn around the paper with the paint for some veggie art!	Bubble Gum Soup! In your chosen plastic bin Mix some water, bath bubbles and pink food coloring! Add some plastic scoops for some fun with bubble gum soup!	Stuff the Turkey! Give your child a big pillow case! Lay out various socks, small stuffed animals, and small pillows Set the timer for 1 minute. Have your child stuff their turkey pillow case as fast as they can!	Turkey Feet! Using pipe cleaners. Help your child twist together some turkey Feet!	Veggie Art! -Brown piece of construction paper -uncooked ear of corn -washable yellow, orange, and red paint Bubble Gum Soup: -pink food coloring Sensory bin: -plastic bin large enough to fit 3 pairs of shoes -water (Always supervise your child when playing with water.) -child friendly

						bath soap for bubbles -pink food coloring -scoops. Stuff the Turkey: -large pillow case -small stuffed animals/rolled socks/ small pillows -timer Turkey Feet: Pipe cleaners
Thursday	Letter of the Week: Ii Number of the Week: 9 Color of the Week: Pink Shape of the Week: Hexagon Your Choice Book!	Thankful Hand prints! Using washable orange/red/brown colors paint the inside of your child's hand! Have them stamp their hand on 5 different times on the	Pumpkin Pie Squish Bag! In a large Ziploc bag add some pumpkin pie filling! Make sure the bag is sealed!	Number Squash! Write down numbers 1-9 on the floor using side walk chalk, or on write them on different sheets of paper, and tape them down (one	Pink Strips! Using a pink construction paper. Practice Cutting! Draw 5 horizontal lines across a pink sheet of	Thankful handprints! -washable paint: brown, yellow, and red, -white construction paper -black marker

		sheet of paper using the different colors! Once the hand prints are dry ask them what they are thankful for. Using a black marker, write down their responses on the handprints!	Tape the bag securely to the table. Have your child practice writing Letters A-I on the squish bag!	number per paper). Have your child hop through numbers 1-9 as they count out loud!	construction paper. Have your child practice cutting using child friendly scissors!	Pumpkin Pie Squish Bag -Large Ziploc bag -pumpkin pie filling -Tape Number Squash: -Sidewalk chalk or if you are working inside: Regular sheets of print/lined paper -tape -marker Practice Cutting! -pink construction paper -black marker to draw lines Pink Strips -Child friendly scissors

| Friday | Letter of the Week: Ii

Number of the Week: 9

Color of the Week: Pink

Shape of the Week: Hexagon

Your Choice Book! | Rock Painting!

Using rocks from your backyard have your child use washable paint and a paint brush to cover them in pink, orange, green, blue, red, yellow, and purple! | Sensory Bin: Potatoes!

Fill your chosen sensory bin with some uncooked potatoes

Questions to ask:

How do they feel?

What color are they?

Are they bumpy? | Shape Race!

Using 3 regular sized papers draw a hexagon, rectangle, and oval.

One shape per sheet of paper.

Make them large enough for your child to see them from across the room.

Tape them to a wall!

In a small container place 9 Sticky notes

3 with a hexagon drawn on

3 with a rectangle

And 3with an oval.

Place them in a container next to your child. | Apple Turkey Snack!

Stick 5 toothpicks on the apple (these will be used as a base for turkey feathers).

Have your child skewer some colorful gum drops using tooth picks. Help them to push their gum drop skewers into their apple to create turkey feathers!

Have your child glue on the two googly eyes and a small piece of orange tissue paper for a turkey beak!

Always supervise your child when working | Rock Art!

-backyard rocks

-washable paint: pink, orange, green, blue, red, yellow, and purple.

-child friendly paint brush

Sensory Bin:

-plastic bin large enough to fit 3 pairs of shoes!

-potatoes (your choice)

Shape Race!

-3 regular sheets of paper

-9 sticky notes

-small container for sticky notes.

Turkey Snack Craft!

-Red Apple |
| --- | --- | --- | --- | --- | --- | --- |

				Set the timer for 1 minute. Have your child race back and forth to retrieve the sticky note to place on the correct shape!	with small objects that may pose choking hazard!	5-9 tooth picks -colorful gum drops -orange tissue paper -googly eyes -glue

Thanksgiving Theme Week: 2

	Circle Time	Craft	Sensory	Gross Motor	Fine Motor	Materials Needed
Monday	Letter of the Week: Jj Number of the Week: 10 Color of the Week: Grey Shape of the Week: Crescent Your Choice Book!	J is for Jelly Beans Using a pink construction paper draw a large letter J (It should take up most of the paper). Have your child decorate by gluing on some jelly beans!	Sensory Bin: Fill your bin with some cranberries and plastic scoops! (Always supervise your child when they are working with small objects)	Catch 10! Play a game of catch using a child friendly bouncy ball! Have your child count to ten as he/she throws and catches the ball!	Clothespin line! Tie a piece of yarn to two chairs! Spread them apart so the yarn does not sag. Give your child some plastic clothespins and have them hang them on the line. Make sure that the chairs you will use will not topple over! Safety First!	J is for Jelly Bean Craft: -pink construction paper -jelly beans Sensory Bin: -plastic container big enough to fit 3 pairs of shoes -cranberries -plastic scoops Always supervise your child when they are working with small objects that may pose choking hazard) Catch 10: Child friendly bouncy ball! Clothespin line: -yarn -two chairs

						-plastic clothespins
Tuesday	Letter of the Week: Jj Number of the Week: 10 Color of the Week: Grey Shape of the Week: Crescent Your Choice Book!	Crescent Moon! Cut some small pieces of aluminum foil On a black piece of construction paper draw a large crescent shape (It should cover most of the page). Have your child glue the aluminum foil onto the crescent shape.	Squish Bag! Fill a large Ziploc bag with shaving cream. Add a few drops of washable black and white paint. Make sure that that the bag is sealed, then tape it to the table, Have your child use their fingers to squish the bag for some non-messy color mixing!	10 Bird Flaps (Jumping Jacks)! Three rounds! Have your child do ten jumping jacks as you help them count!	On a piece of construction paper write down the letter "Jj" in multiple areas of the paper (minimum of 10 times) Give your child a grey crayon. Have them color each letter J.	Crescent Moon Craft: -aluminum foil -Black construction paper -glue Squish Bag -Ziploc bag -shaving cream -washable black and white paint -tape -10 Bird Flaps Just your sweet encouraging voice as you help them count to 10!
Wednesday	Letter of the Week: Jj Number of the Week:10 Color of the Week: Grey Shape of the Week : Crescent	Number 10 cranberry Craft! Write down the number ten on a piece of construction paper. It should be at least half the	Sensory Bin: Fill your bowl with: -dry pasta -plastic measuring cups -plastic bowls.	Water Balloon Color Splash! Fill up some water balloons! Go outside! Using side walk chalk draw	Turkey Toes! Have your child use a plastic spoon to fill a small sandwich bag with some candy corn! Tell them they are turkey toes!	Number 10 cranberry craft: -pen/marker construction paper -cranberries -glue Sensory Bin:

	Your Choice Book!	size of the sheet! Have your child trace the number 10 with glue and cranberries As they are gluing the cranberries have them practice counting to 10.		different color circles. Have your child identify the different colors on the ground! Once they have identified a color have them toss and splash the balloon on that specific color! Indoor: If you are working indoors draw and color in the circles on different pieces of paper. Instead of balloons use bouncy balls or rolled up socks!	When they are done tie the bag with a ribbon and have them give it to a special friend that they are thankful for!	-plastic bin large enough to fit 3 pairs of shoes! -dry pasta -plastic bowls –plastic measuring cups (Always supervise your child when they are working with small items that may pose choking hazard.) Water Balloon Splash: -water balloons -sidewalk chalk -bucket to hold balloons If you are working indoors: -bouncy balls/rolled up socks -paper -colors/markers

						-container to hold bouncy balls or socks Turkey Toes! -plastic spoon -sandwich bag -ribbon
Thursday	Letter of the Week: Jj Number of the Week:10 Color of the Week: Grey Shape of the Week: Crescent Your Choice Book!	Yam Buddies! Using washable paint have your child paint a yam! Have them glue on two googly eyes. Have them tape on some precut yarn hair! Finally help them to draw on a smile using a marker!	Sensory Bin: Fill your bin with some fuzzy pom-poms and child friendly tweezers	Turkey Feather bubble pop! Give your child a colorful piece of tissue paper. It should be long enough to flap in the wind and catch bubbles! Blow some bubbles and have your child run to pop each bubble with their turkey feather!	Letters A-J Review On a piece of white construction paper write down letters A a– Jj Have your child practice identifying each letter. As they identify each letter have them glue on a popcorn kernel (Always supervise your child when they are working with small objects).	Yam Buddies! -Yam -washable paint (child's choice). -googly eyes -precut strands of yarn -tape -marker Sensory Bin: Plastic bin large enough to fit 3 pairs of shoes -fuzzy pom poms (always supervise your child when playing with small objects that may pose

						choking hazard) -child friendly tweezers. Turkey Feather Bubble Pop: -Bubbles -Feather (colorful tissue paper big enough to catch and pop bubbles!) Letters A-J Review - white construction paper -glue -un-popped kernels of popcorn (Always supervise your child when working with small items that may pose choking hazard) -pen/marker to write down letters
Friday	Letter of the Week: Jj	Pumpkin Pie Art! Have your child use a	Sensory Bin Fill your bin with some dry beans and	ABC Balloon Tennis! Using a child friendly	Coloring Fun! Trace your child's hands	Pumpkin Pie Art -paper plate

	Number of the Week: 10 Color of the Week: Grey Shape of the Week: Crescent Your Choice Book!	paint brush and some orange washable paint to completely cover the inside of a paper plate. Have them dip their fingers in washable brown finger paint, then have them stamp their fingers along the edge to make the crust!	alphabet letter magnets (A-J) Have your child practice identifying each letter. (Always supervise your child when playing with small objects that may pose choking hazard).	racket play a game of tennis using a balloon! As you play say the ABCs as you and your child hit the balloon with your rackets!	piece of paper. Help them to trace your hand as well. Have your child color the hand prints using their favorite colors!	-washable orange paint -brown washable finger paint -paint brush Sensory Bin: -dry Beans -Child Learning ABC Magnets (If you do not have ABC magnets write down letters A-J on pieces on sticky notes. Mix the sticky notes in with the beans!) ABC Balloon Tennis -Child friendly racket -balloon Coloring Fun -Paper -Crayons

Thanksgiving Theme Week: 3

	Circle Time	Craft	Sensory	Gross Motor	Fine Motor	Materials Needed
Monday	Letter of the Week: Kk

Number of the Week :11

Color of the Week: Blue

Shape of the Week: Semi circle

Your Choice Book! | Kite Craft

Cut a diamond shape out of a regular sheet of print paper

Have your child decorate their kite using their favorite character stickers (superhero, teddy bear, etc.)

Using a hole puncher make a hole in the front corner of the kite big enough to string a piece of yarn.

 Tie one side of the string to the kite and the other side to a popsicle stick (this is | Sensory Bin: Thanksgiving dinner dish wash!

-bubble bath bubbles

-play pots and pans

-water

-child friendly dish brush. | Fly a kite!

Have an outdoor day running and flying kites! | Mini Marshmallow Count!

Give your child two containers.

One container will be filled with mini marshmallows and the other will be empty.

Have your child transfer the mini marshmallows to the empty container using child friendly tweezers.

As they are transferring the marshmallows have them practice counting to 11. | Kit Craft:

-regular sheet of white paper

-character Stickers

-popsicle stick.

-hole puncher

-yarn

Sensory Bin: Thanksgiving dinner dish wash

-plastic bin large enough to fit 3 pairs of shoes

-child friendly bath bubbles

-child's play dishes

-child friendly dish brush

Fly a Kite: |

		your kite handle).				You can use a purchased kite or you can run and play with your child's kite craft! Mini Marshmallow Count: -two empty plastic bowl/containers -child friendly tweezers -mini marshmallows
Tuesday	Letter of the Week: Kk Number of the Week 11 Color of the Week: Blue Shape of the Week: Semi circle Your Choice Book!	Blue Semi Circle: Cut a paper plate in half Have your child dip their finger in some washable blue paint, then have them paint their semi-circle by dotting their fingers throughout the inside	Blue Sensory Bin: Add blue child friendly items to your sensory bin: Example - blue plastic cups -blue plastic plates -blue pillow cases	Fall Football fun! Play a game of catch using a child friendly football!	Tissue Snips! Have your child practice cutting using child friendly scissors and tissue paper!	Blue Semi Circle: -Washable blue finger paint -half paper plate Blue Sensory Bin: -plastic sensory bin big enough to fit 3 pairs of shoes -Your choice of

		area of the shape!	-blue stuffed animals -blue shirts!			child friendly blue items! (Always supervise your child when playing with small items. Fall Football Fun! -child friendly football Tissue Snips -Colorful tissue paper 1-2 sheets (Save the cut tissue paper for later use) -Child Friendly Scissors
Wednesday	Letter of the Week: Kk Number of the Week: 11 Color of the Week: Blue Shape of the Week: Semi circle	Owl Craft! -Give your child a pinecone! -Precut a very small triangle using an orange construction paper. This will be used	Squish Bag Using a black marker write down letters Hh Ii Jj Kk	Jump over Using side walk chalk draw a line. On either side of the line write down numbers 1-11	Number Practice with Clothespins On the sides a piece of clean cardboard. down 1-11 Then place one plastic clothespin	Owl Craft! -pine Cone -washable blue paint -googly eyes -orange construction paper

		as the owl's beak! Have your child use washable blue paint and a paintbrush paint their pinecone. Once the paint is dry help your child to glue two googly eyes and the triangle beak to the pinecone!	One letter in each of the corners of the bag. Fill your bag with Clear hair gel and 5 water beads Make sure that the bag is tightly sealed. Tape it onto the table! Have your child move the beads around to the different corners. Have them identify the letters as they maneuver all of the beads to that corner.	Alternate the numbers on each side of the line. 1 on the left 2 on the right 3 on the left 4 on the right etc. Have the child jump over the line until they reach number 11. Make sure to count out loud as they are jumping!	on top of each of the numbers. Have your child remove the clothespins. As they remove the clothespin have them practice identifying the numbers.	-glue -paintbrush Water Bead Squish Bag -hair gel -water beads 5 - Ziploc bag -tape -black marker Jump Over: Sidewalk chalk If you are doing this activity inside: Write the numbers down on paper and tape them down securely. Use yarn to create the line! Number Practice with clothespins: -flat cardboard

					-pen/marker -plastic clothespins (Always supervise your child when working with small items.)
Thursday	Letter of the Week: Kk Number of the Week 11 Color of the Week: Blue Shape of the Week: Semi circle Your Choice Book!	Friendly Scarecrow Mask: -precut some yellow yarn strands for some straw scarecrow hair -precut a blue triangle using blue construction paper for scarecrow hat! Using a paper plate Have your child glue on two buttons for the eyes Next have them glue	Play Dough Cookies Give your child a child friendly rolling pin, and some child friendly cookie cutters. Have them put on an apron and a chef's hat!	Fall Bike Ride! Go outside for a bike ride! Take a look at all the Fall Trees!	Leaf Match On a piece of regular paper write down letters Aa-Kk Using a black marker write down letters Aa-Kk on some collected leaves. Have your child play a game of match with the letters!	Friendly Scarecrow Mask: Paper plate -washable orange and red paint -yellow yarn strands -2 buttons -glue -blue construction paper -popsicle stick (this is your mask handle). (Always supervise our child when working with small objects)

91

| | | on the blue hat

, then have them add the yellow yarn hair to the sides!

Using washable finger paint have your child leave an orange finger paint nose

And have them brush on a big red smile !

Once they are done glue the top of the popsicle stick to the bottom of the backside of the plate. This is your mask handle. | | | | Play Dough Cookies

-child friendly cookie cutters

-child friendly rolling pin

-child friendly cookie cutters

-chef hat

Fall Bike Ride:

-Tricycle

Leaf Match Activity:

-leaves

-paper

-marker |
| Friday | Letter of the Week: Kk

Number of the Week:11

Color of the | Fall Leaf Wreathes

Cut a circle inside a paper plate so that only | Sensory Bin

Fill your bin with the following: | Fall Hike!

Go outdoors for a fun family Fall hike around the | Write your child's name in broken lines------ | Fall Wreathe

-paper plate

-washable red/yellow/o |

	Week: Blue Shape of the Week: Semi circle Your Choice Book!	the edges of the plate remain. Have your child Use washable red/orange/yellow and brown paint to fully cover the base of the wreath. Once the paint is dry have your child glue on some big fall leaves!	-kinetic sand -plastic scoops!	neighborhood. As you are walking around have your child collect some beautiful Fall treasures: leaves and pinecones.	Give your child a blue crayon and have them practice tracing their name.	range/brown paint -kid friendly paint brush -Big Fall leaves -Glue Sensory Bin: -plastic bin big enough to fit 3 pairs of shoes. -kinetic play sand - plastic scoops Fall Hike: Walking shoes -small bag to carry Fall treasures! Name Tracing: -regular print paper -blue crayon

Thanksgiving Theme Week 4

	Circle Time	Craft	Sensory	Gross Motor	Fine Motor	Materials needed
Monday	Letter of the Week: Ll Number of the Week :12 Color of the Week: Red Shape of the Week: Octagon Your Choice Book!	L is for Leaf Have your child use some washable red paint to brush some Fall leaves. Once they are done have them press their leaves on a yellow sheet of construction paper to make some leaf prints!	Sensory Bin Fill your Sensory bin with some Fall Pinecones of different sizes Questions to ask: Which is bigger? How does it feel? What color is it?	Bull's-eye! Set down a hula hoop across the room. Give them some bean bags! Have them practice tossing the bean bags so that they land in the center of the hula hoop!	Corn Kernels Transfer Activity: Give your child some corn kernels. Have them use child friendly tweezers or a plastic spoon to move the kernels from their original plastic bowl to an empty bowl. Have them practice counting to 12 as they transfer the kernels.	L is for Leaf Craft: -washable red paint -large Fall Leaf -child friendly paint brush -yellow construction paper. Sensory Bin: -plastic bin big enough to fit 3 pairs of shoes -Pinecones different sizes Bulls Eye: -hula hoop -bean bags Corn Kernel Transfer Activity: -dry corn kernels

						-child friendly tweezers or plastic spoon -2 plastic bowls
Tuesday	Letter of the Week: Ll Number of the Week: 12 Color of the Week: Red Shape of the Week: Octagon Your Choice Book!	Draw an Octagon on a black piece of construction paper Have your child trace the lines of the shape with glue. Next have them glue dry spaghetti sticks for some fun pasta art!	Red Fizzy Fun! In a plastic container add about ½ cup of baking soda In a separate container mix some white vinegar and red food coloring. Fill some child friendly pipettes with the mixture. Next help your child squeeze the pipette onto the baking soda! Enjoy	Fruit basket switch! Place a container across the room filled with your choice of 4 apples or oranges. Have your child lunge across the room while holding an apple/orange to the sky! Once they get to the container have them place the red apple in the container. Have them take an orange/apple from the other	Fine Motor Play dough Worms and Letters! On a piece of regular sheet paper draw a large letter "L" (It should take up the full page). Have your child roll out pieces of playdough (think worm shape) to trace the lines of the letter!	Octagon Craft: -black construction paper -glue -dry spaghetti noodles Red Fizzy Fun: -child Friendly pipettes -baking soda -white vinegar -red food coloring -2 plastic containers -mat

			the fizzy fun! This activity can get messy so make sure to lay down a mat and supervise your child at all times)	container and lunge back across the room until all the fruits have been transferred to different containers! (Rolled different colored socks also work great for this activity!		Fruit Basket Switch: -2 Baskets -4 oranges -4 apples Or if you are out of fruit choose different colored socks as stand in for the fruit. Play dough Worms and Letters Activity: -Regular sheet of print paper -Play dough (color of the week is preferable for review).
Wednesday	Letter of the Week: Ll Number of the Week 12 Color of the Week: Red	12 Red Apples on a Tree! You will need a piece of construction paper	Sensory Play: Fill your bin with the following: -water	Mini Hoops! Give your child some ping pong balls. Set up 4 cups.	Lego Towers! Have your child build Lego towers using 12 building blocks!	12 Red Apples on a tree craft: -washable brown and green paint

	Shape of the Week : Octagon Your Choice Book!	(yellow/white) Using washable brown paint, help your child paint a tree trunk and branches! Then using washable green paint, have your child paint some leaves! Once the paint is dry, have your child dip their finger in some red finger paint! Have them stamp some red apples on the tree 12 total! Make sure to count them!	-bath tub toys -bubble bath bubbles!	On each cup draw a different shape. Octagon Rectangle Oval Triangle Before each toss have them identify the name of the shape!	Make sure to count as they build the tower!	-child friendly paint brush -red finger paint -piece of yellow/white construction paper. Sensory Bin: -plastic tub large enough to fit 3 pairs of shoes -bath bubbles -bath toys -water Always supervise your child when playing with water or small objects that may pose choking hazard. Mini Hoops: -Ping Pong balls

						-Plastic Cubs -Marker to draw shapes Lego Towers: Lego building blocks
Thursday	Letter of the Week: Ll Number of the Week :12 Color of the Week: Red Shape of the Week: Octagon Your Choice Book!	Water Bottle Turkey Craft: -Precut a small piece of orange tissue paper (for the beak) Have your child tear pieces of brown tissue paper. -Have them glue the torn pieces on a water bottle. Make sure the bottle is	Sensory Bin: -plastic measuring cups -large plastic Spoon -plastic Bowl -Oatmeal	Play a game of Color Tag with your child! -Wear some old shirts and pants! Dip your fingers in some orange/yell ow/red washable paint! Whatever color you and your child choose make sure to yell it out when you tag! Red tag/Yellow/	Counting with pom poms: On a plastic cup draw numbers 2, 5, 8, 12. Give your child some colorful pom poms. Have them use child friendly tweezers to drop the correct number of pom poms into each cup! (Always supervise	Turkey Water Bottle Craft: -Empty water bottle -googly eyes -colorful feathers -brown tissue paper -small piece of orange tissue paper -glue Sensory Bin: -plastic bin big enough to fit 3 pairs of shoes

		fully covered -Have them glue on two googly eyes -Have them take a small piece of orange tissue paper and glue it on as the beak! -Have them glue some colorful feathers to the back of the bottle!		orange tag etc. Have some colorful fun!	your child when working with small objects).	-plastic large spoon -plastic measuring cups -plastic small bowls. -oatmeal Counting with pom poms: -fuzzy pom poms -child friendly tweezers -plastic cups -marker to draw on numbers Color Tag: -red/orange/yellow washable finger paint -Old pants and shirts!
Friday	Letter of the Week: L l	Squash Painting! Have your child use washable	Sensory Bin: Fill your bin with the following:	Bouncy Ball Square! Draw for large squares on	Trace 12 with pom poms! On a regular sheet of	Squash painting -washable paint(red, yellow,

Number of the Week 12: Color of the Week: Red Shape of the Week: Octagon	paint to decorate a large squash! Give them a variety of choice colors!	-acorns -scoops -shovels	the ground using sidewalk chalk. Inside one square draw a large letter "Ll" In the second square draw the number 12. In the third square draw an octagon. In the fourth square draw a triangle. Ask your child where is the number 12? Have them bounce their ball of the 12 Ask where is the triangle? Have them bounce the ball of the triangle.	paper draw a large number 12. It should take up at least half the sheet. Give your child some fuzzy pom poms. Have them trace the lines of the number 12 using glue and pom poms.	orange, brown) -child friendly paint brush Large Squash (Your choice) Sensory Bin: -Plastic bin big enough to fit 3 pairs of shoes -acorns -plastic shovels -scoops Bouncy Ball square: -sidewalk chalk -bouncy ball (If you are completing this activity indoors use painters tape to create the square. Write down the number, letter, and

| | | | | They can bounce the ball or they can hop to the correct answer while holding the bouncy ball. | | shapes on a piece of paper and then tape the paper securely to the floor.) Trace 12 with pom poms -regular sheet of paper -fuzzy pom poms -glue |

Christmas Theme Week: 1

	Circle Time	Craft	Sensory	Gross Motor	Fine Motor	Materials Needed
Monday	Letter of the Week: Mm

Number of the Week: 13

Color of the Week: Green

Shape of the Week: Star

Your Choice Book! | M is for Mouse:

Precut a small pink triangle (mouse nose)

Using washable grey paint, paint the bottom of your child's foot.

Place their foot on a white piece of construction paper.

The heel of their foot print will be the face of the mouse.

Using a small paint brush draw on two circles on either side for ears. | Sensory Play:

Set out a plastic mat on the table!

-premade cookie dough

-child friendly rolling pin

-child friendly cookie cutters | Santa's Bag!

Give your child a large pillow case!

Place small stuffed animals around the room!

Set the timer for 1 minute!

Have them race around the room collecting all of the toys as fast as they can before the timer chimes! | Christmas Paper Snip!

Give your child some Christmas theme gift wrapping paper.

Have them practice cutting the paper using child friendly scissors. | M is for Mouse:

Washable grey paint

-white construction paper

-small paint brush

-small pink construction paper triangle

-glue

-googly eyes

Santa's Bag

-timer

-large pillow case

-small stuffed animals

Cookie Dough Squish!

-premade cookie dough |

		Once the paint has dried have your child glue on 2 googly eyes a pink construction paper triangle nose. Help them to draw on whiskers.				-child friendly rolling pin -child friendly cookie cutters Christmas Paper Snip: -Christmas theme wrapping paper -Child friendly scissors
Tuesday	Letter of the Week: Mm Number of the Week :13 Color of the Week: Green Shape of the Week: Star Your Choice Book!	Pine Trees! Using a piece of construction paper draw a large triangle. The triangle should take up more than half of the sheet. Have your child dip a plastic fork in some washable green paint, then have	Sensory Bin Fill your bin with the following: -ice -child friendly tweezers - if available add some artic theme plastic polar bears/ penguins (Always supervise your child	Penguin Belly slide Tie a long piece of yarn to your child's favorite blanket (The string should reach across the floor.) Next have your child place their favorite stuffed animal on	Peppermint Stick writing practice Using a plate or tray fill the bottom with salt. Have your child use a peppermint stick to practice drawing letters A-M -Always place a mat around the work area	Pine Trees" - construction paper -washable green paint -plastic fork Sensory Bin: Plastic bin big enough to fit 3 pairs of shoes -ice cubes (enough to fill bottom of the bin!

		them stamp the fork inside the triangle to create some green pine needles!	when playing with small objects.)	the blanket belly down. Have your child stand across the room from their blanket. Give your child the other end of the string that is attached to the blanket across the room. Tell them that they have to help their penguin belly slide over! Set the stopwatch! Have them reel their penguin in as fast as they can!	to avoid added clean up!	-artic theme plastic toys (Always supervise your child when playing with small objects). -child friendly tweezers Penguin Belly Slide: -Child's favorite blanket -yarn -Child's favorite stuffed animal -stopwatch Peppermint stick writing practice: -paper plate or plastic tray -salt -mat to avoid added clean up.

| Wednesday | Letter of the Week: Mm

Number of the Week: 13

Color of the Week: Green

Shape of the Week: Star

Your Choice Book! | Star Craft

Using a black piece of construction paper draw a large star. The star should be larger than half of the paper.

Have your child tear pieces of yellow tissue paper.

Have them glue the pieces onto the star so that the shape is fully covered. | Sensory Bin

Fill your bin with the following:

-jingle bells

-child friendly magnet wand | Christmas music dance party!

Have a dance party with your child!

Dance to some fun Christmas theme music! | 13 stars!

Using a piece of black construction paper as a base, use a white chalk to write the number 13 in multiple places on the sheet of paper (13 times) Make sure to spread them out!

Have your child dip their finger into some white washable paint, then have them touch the number with their paint covered finger!

When you are done help them count the stars! | Star Shape Craft:

-black Construction paper

-yellow Tissue paper

Sensory Bin:

Jingle Bells

-child friendly magnet wand

Christmas music dance party!

-fast fun Christmas music!

13 Stars

-white finger paint

-black construction paper

-white chalk |
|---|---|---|---|---|---|

Thursday	Letter of the Week: Mm

Number of the Week :13

Color of the

Week: Green

Shape of the Week:

Star

Your Choice Book! | Santa's Beard Craft!

Cut a paper plate in half

Have your child glue cotton balls on the plate. Make sure the plate is fully covered.

Finally Glue a popsicle stick to the round bottom portion of the plate!

Have your child hold up their Santa Beard to their face! | Disappearing peppermint stripes!

In a small plastic container add some warm milk

Have your child use some kid friendly tweezers to place peppermint candy sticks in the warm milk.

Have them smell the peppermint before placing it in the milk.

Have them watch the stripes melt away! | Snow Ball Fight!

Roll up some white socks and have a pretend snow ball fight! | Santa's Work Shop!

Have your child put together some pretend toys using bristle blocks or Legos! | Santa's Beard Craft

-paper plate

-glue

-cotton balls

-popsicle stick

Disappearing peppermint stripes:

-small plastic container

-warm milk (always check temperature to make sure it's not too hot!)

-peppermint candy sticks

-child friendly tweezers!

Santa's Workshop!

-Bristle Blocks or Legos |

						Snow Ball Fight! -Rolled Socks
Friday	Letter of the Week: Mm Number of the Week :13 Color of the Week: Green Shape of the Week: Star Your Choice Book!	Christmas Wreathe Use a paper plate! Precut the middle section out. You should be left with just the border of the plate! Have your child tear red and green tissue paper! Have then glue on the mixture of red and green tissue paper on to the paper plate. Make it so the plate is fully covered in festive colors!	Sensory Bin Fill your bin with the following: -walnuts -scoops	Santa Race! Using side walk chalk draw a line write down numbers 1-13 on one side of the line. Have your child race as fast as they can through the line as they count out loud! Have them wear a Santa hat! Tell them to pretend they are Santa running from house to house! 13 houses total!	Pasta friendship bracelets! Have your child thread some rigatoni pasta using some pipe cleaners! Once they have finished threading the pasta, help them to tie the ends together!	Christmas Wreathe -red and green tissue paper -glue -scissors -paper plate Sensory Bin: -plastic bin large enough to fit 3 pairs of shoes -walnuts -scoops Pasta Friendship Bracelet -Rigatoni pasta pipe cleaners Santa Race

						-sidewalk chalk
						If you are doing this activity inside use painter's tape and write the numbers down on different sheets of paper.
						Secure the paper down with tape.
						-Santa Hat

Christmas Theme Week: 2

	Circle Time	Craft	Sensory	Gross Motor	Fine Motor	Materials Needed
Monday	Letter of the Week: Nn Number of the Week :14 Color of the Week: Yellow Shape of the Week: Heptagon Your Choice Book!	N is For Nest Have your child tear some brown tissue paper. Have them glue the pieces of tissue paper around a paper plate bowl so that the outside and inside of the bowl is fully covered. Give your child a hard boil egg to place inside!	Christmas Sensory Bin -Child friendly ornaments -tinsel -jingle bells	Jingle Bell Dance! Give your child some jingle bell bracelets. Place them on their hands and feet! Play their favorite holiday fast song! For 30 seconds at a time! Have them dance and shake the bells as fast as they can! Set the timer for some jingle bell fun!	Magnets and Jingle Bells! Set up a big bowl with jingle bells inside! Have your child use a magnet wand transfer the metal bells over to a different container!	N is for Nest! -brown tissue paper -glue -paper plate bowl -hardboiled egg! Sensory Bin: -plastic Bin large enough to fit 3 pairs of shoes -child friendly ornaments -tinsel -jingle bells (Always supervise your child when working or playing with small objects that may pose

						choking hazard.) Jingle Bell Dance! -jingle bell bracelets -favorite fast holiday song! -timer Magnets and Jingle Bells! -child friendly magnet wand -metal jingle bells -bowl
Tuesday	Letter of the Week: Nn Number of the Week: 14 Color of the Week: Yellow	Shapes and Patterns Draw a large Heptagon on a piece of construction paper! Have your child count the sides	Ornament Wash! Fill the tub with some - water -bath -dish washing child	Clear the Snow! Create a Shovel out of an empty paper towel tube and a piece of construction paper! Tape them securely	Build 14 Place 14 straws in a plastic container! Have your child transfer the straw to a different container	Shapes and Patterns - construction Paper -red and green pom poms -glue

Shape of the Week : Heptagon Your Choice Book!	and the corners! Have them trace each side with glue and then have them glue fuzzy green and red pom poms along the sides of the Heptagon! Alternate the colors so that they create a pattern! Ask your child what color should go next?	friendly brush —plastic scoops -bubble bath bubbles -plastic ornaments	together so that they form a shovel! Spread some cotton balls around the floor! Set the timer for 30 seconds Have your child collect as many cotton balls as they can before the time runs out! Make sure to play some holiday music throughout the activity!	using their fingers. Have them count the straws as they are being transferred. Help them place the straws on the floor so they create the number 14.	Ornament Wash Sensory Bin: -plastic bin large enough to fit 3 pairs of shoes. -Bath bubbles -plastic child friendly ornaments -water -brush -scoops Always supervise your child when playing with water or working with small objects that may pose choking hazard. Clear the Snow! -paper towel tube

						-construction paper -tape -cotton balls -holiday music -timer Build 14 -14 Straws -plastic container -plastic straws
Wednesday	Letter of the Week: Nn Number of the Week :14 Color of the Week: Yellow Shape of the Week: Heptagon Your Choice Book!	Handprint Christmas trees! Using washable green paint finger paint, cover your child's palm and fingers! Have them place their hand on a piece of yellow construction paper!	Sensory Bin: Fill your bin with walnuts and scoops	Match the letter! Write letters "Hh" through "Nn" on different pieces of paper. Tape the papers on the wall Have your child stand across the room from	Puzzles Help your child put together their favorite puzzle!	Handprint Christmas Trees: -yellow construction paper -washable finger paints: green, red, blue, purple -gold star sticker Sensory Bin: -plastic bin large enough to

| | | They should leave green handprint trees!

Have them decorate their tree with red, purple, and blue finger prints!

When they are done finger painting add a gold star sticker to the top of the tree! | | the wall of letters.

Place sticky note cards with matching letters next to the child.

Have the child take a sticky note and race across the room. Once they have reached the wall have them place the sticky note on the matching letter.

Have them race back and forth until all the letters have been matched! | | fit 3 pairs of shoes

-walnuts

-scoops

Always supervise your child when playing with small objects that may pose choking hazard.

Match the letter!

-regular sized paper

-tape

-sticky notes

-
pen/marker

Puzzles:

Your child's favorite puzzle! |
| Thursday | Letter of the Week: Nn | Paint a snow storm with bubble wrap! | Sensory Bottle: Glitter and Water! | The Grinch stole Christmas! | Snow Man Stuffing!

Use a black marker to | Paint a Snow Storm with Bubble Wrap |

	Number of the Week :14 Color of the Week: Yellow Shape of the Week: Heptagon Your Choice Book!	Have your child paint a bubble wrap sheet white! Once the sheet is covered in white have them flip the sheet over and press it onto a black piece of construction paper. Have them repeat this process until the black construction is filled with white prints!	Fill a water bottle a little less than full. Add a few drops of silver glitter. Make sure the water bottle is sealed tight!	Place child friendly ornaments and gift bows around the house! Give your child a big pillow case. Set the timer to 1 minute Have them run around the house collecting all the Christmas items as fast as they can! Give them some green mittens and a Santa hat to wear!	draw on two eyes and a happy face on a bottle. Use an orange marker to draw on a carrot nose! Give your child a bowl full of cotton balls! Have them push the cotton balls inside the water bottle until it is entirely full!	-washable white paint -Child friendly paint brush -black construction paper Sensory Bottle: -water bottle -silver glitter -water The Grinch Stole Christmas! -pillow Case -child friendly ornaments -gift bows -green mittens -Santa hat -timer

| Friday | Letter of the Week: Nn

Number of the Week :14

Color of the Week: Yellow

Shape of the Week: Heptagon

Your Choice Book! | Ornament Painting!

Have your child decorate their own ornament!

Choose a clear ornament (plastic)

Give your child some washable paint and a child friendly small brush. Have them decorate their ornament with their choice of colors! | Sensory Bin

Fill your bin with the following:

-fake snow

-plastic scoops

-artic theme toys | Pillow Snowman!

Use Big pillows, hats, and scarfs to build a pretend snow man! | Fruit Loop Shape Tracing!

Using any color construction paper draw a star, a heptagon, and rectangle. They should be about the size of your hand. Easy for your child to trace.

Have your child trace the sides of the shapes with glue.

Next have them glue on some fruit loops! | Ornament Painting

-Plastic Ornament

-washable paint

-small brush

Sensory Bin:

Plastic Bin large enough to fit 3 pairs of shoes

(Always supervise your child when working with small objects that may pose choking hazard.)

-fake Snow (you can make your own recipe, use cotton balls, or use store bought.)

-artic Themed toys: penguins, |
|---|---|---|---|---|---|

						polar bears, walrus
						-scoops
						Pillow Snowman:
						-big fluffy pillows
						-hats
						-scarves
						Fruit Loop Shape Tracing
						-Fruit Loops
						-glue
						-construction paper
						-marker to draw shapes

Christmas Theme Week: 3

	Circle Time	Craft	Sensory	Gross Motor	Fine Motor	Material Needed
Monday	Letter of the Week: Oo Number of the Week :15 Color of the Week: Brown Shape of the Week: Nonagon Your Choice Book!	O is for Octopus(handprint craft) Using washable purple finger paint the inside of your child's hand, then have them press their hand down on blue construction paper. Add on 3 more octopus arms using a small brush so that you have a total of 8. Once the paint has dried have your child glue on some cheerios to the tentacles!	Melted Snow Man! In a Ziploc bag add two googly eyes, a baby carrot, and 5 raisins! Fill the bag with water. Make sure it sealed and tape it to the table! Have your child have some non-messy melted snowman squish fun!	Zig Zag Hockey Use painter's tape to create a zig zag pattern across the room! Give your child a rolled up pair of socks. Give your child a child size hockey stick or a clean toy broom! Have your child play a game of zig zag hockey across the room!	Build a Nonagon Using painter's tape create a nonagon shape on the ground Have your child use Legos to trace the shape!	O is for Octopus! -washable purple paint -paintbrush -blue construction paper -cheerios -glue -googly eyes Melted Snowman! -Ziploc bag -googly eyes -5 raisins -baby carrot -tape -water Zig Zag Hockey -Rolled up socks -painter's tape

		Don't forget to also glue on some googly eyes!			-child size hockey stick or clean toy broom! Build a Nonagon! Lego's -painter's tape
Tuesday	Letter of the Week: Oo Number of the Week :15 Color of the Week: Brown Shape of the Week: Nonagon Your Choice Book!	Winter Trees! Using a piece of blue construction paper draw 3 large Letter Y. These are your tree trunk and branches! Have your child use a small paint brush to trace the trees with some washable brown paint! Next have them dip their finger in some	What is that Holiday Scent? Have your child cover their eyes. See if they can identify some holiday smells! -Have them smell a pine scent -Have them smell some cinnamon sticks -Have them smell some fresh baked cookies!	Ornaments and Numbers Using painter's tape create a large triangle on the floor! On different pieces of paper write down numbers 10-15 and tape them down securely on the inside of the triangle. Give your child some multicolor socks or bean bags.	Decorate some Christmas cookies! Give you're plain sugar cookie. Also some icing and some sprinkles! Have them decorate their cookie!	Winter Trees! -washable brown paint -blue construction paper -washable white finger paint! -black marker to draw Y What is that Holiday Scent? - A fresh pine smell (Christmas trees work perfect!) -cinnamon sticks

| | | white finger paint!

Guide their fingers to create snow on the trees and on the ground! | | Tell them that they must hit the numbers on the tree using pretend ornaments! | | -fresh baked cookies

Christmas Cookies!

-plain sugar cookie

-store bought Icing

-sprinkles (holiday colors work best!)

Ornaments and Numbers!

-painter's tape

-paper regular sized

-marker to draw numbers

-tape

If you are doing this activity outdoors all you need is sidewalk chalk! |

| Wednesday | Letter of the Week: Oo

Number of the Week :15

Color of the Week: Brown

Shape of the Week: Nonagon

Your Choice Book! | Ginger Bread House decorated with shapes

Using a brown sheet of construction paper draw a large pentagon at least half of the sheet.

-using red, green, and yellow construction paper cut out small triangles, squares, ovals, rectangles, circles.

Have your child decorate their gingerbread house using glue and the colorful shapes! | Holiday Sounds!

Have your child cover their eyes!

Have them listen to the following:

- jingle bells

- Santa's laugh!

-Santa's Footsteps (Stomp your Feet while wearing boots!)

-Tear some wrapping paper! | Ornament Toss!

Cut 3 big holes into a poster paper!

Color around the first hole red, the second hole green, and the third blue

Have your child take aim and toss rolled socks or small balls into each of the holes!

Have them identify the color of the hole before they take aim! | Christmas Yarn Ball!

Use a paper plate!

Use a hole punch to create holes along the sides and middle of the plate!

-Give your child some red and green yarn!

Have them lace the plate so that it is fully covered in holiday colors! | Ginger Bread Shape House!

-brown, red, green, and yellow construction paper.

-glue

-scissors

Holiday Sounds

-wrapping paper

-recording of Santa's laugh

-boots

-jingle bells

Christmas Yarn Ball

-paper plate

-red and green yarn

-hole punch

Ornament Toss: |
|---|---|---|---|---|---|

						Rolled socks or small balls
						-Red, Green, Blue marker or crayons
						-poster paper or cardboard box
						-box cutter or scissor (whatever is easiest to cut holes).
Thursday	Letter of the Week: Oo

Number of the Week :15

Color of the

Week: Brown

Shape of the Week:

Nonagon

Your Choice Book! | Snow Flake Handprints!

Using washable paint/finger paint, cover the inside of child's hand in white washable paint.

Have them stamp their hand on a piece of blue constructio n paper. | Sensory Bin: Reindeer Food!

-oatmeal

-plastic funnels

-plastic toy deer | Chimney Hop!

Using hula hoops place 4 hula hoops on the ground next to each other. If you do not have hula hoops use painter's tape to create squares.

Tell your child that they are Santa | Mini Christmas Tree!

Have your child use pom poms to decorate a mini craft tree! The pom poms should easily stick to the bristles of the craft tree! | Snow Flake Handprints

-blue constructio n paper

-washable white finger paint

-

Sensory Bin:

-plastic Bin large enough to fit 3 pairs of shoes

-dry oatmeal |

		Leave a total of 3 hand prints Have them count their fingers! Then have them dip one finger in the paint and stamp around their hand prints to add smaller snowflakes!		Clause and that they must hop from chimney to chimney!		-toy plastic deer -plastic funnels Chimney Hop! -Hula Hoops or Painter's Tape Mini Christmas Tree! -Pom poms -mini craft tree Sensory Bin:
Friday	Letter of the Week: Oo Number of the Week :15 Color of the Week: Brown Shape of the Week: Nonagon Your Choice Book!	Snowy number mountain! On a piece of brown construction paper draw multiple number 15s. -Give your child a bowl full of cotton balls. Have your child glue	Sensory Bin: Bowl full of Jelly Red/ Green Jell-O -plastic spoons and small bowls!	Play Snow Ball! You will need some rolled up white socks and plastic bat Use white print paper for bases. Make sure they are taped securely to the floor.	Letter O Art! Give your child some washable green, red, blue, and purple paint! Have them dip an empty roll of toilet paper in the paint! Then have them stamp	Snowy Number Mountain! -brown construction paper -cotton balls -glue -tape Bowl full of Jelly! -Plastic sensory bin big enough

		the cotton balls on each of the number 15s. Once the cotton has dried shape the paper into a cone so that the cotton balls are on the outside of the cone, then tape it to maintain the shape! You have created a snowy Mountain!		Also make sure that your play area is free of any breakables or tripping hazards! If you live in warm weather feel free to play outdoors!	the top of roll onto a piece of brown construction paper! Have them cover the paper in the letter O.	to fit 3 pairs of shoes! -green/red Jell-O -plastic spoons -plastic small bowls Always supervise your child when playing with anything that could potentially pose a choking hazard. Play Snowball -Rolled socks -child friendly bat! -white paper -tape Letter O Art -Construction paper -Washable paint:

						green, red, purple, blue
						-empty toilet paper roll.

Christmas Theme Week: 4

	Circle Time	Craft	Sensory	Gross Motor	Fine Motor	Materials needed
Monday	Letter of the Week: Pp

Number of the Week: 16

Color of the Week: Pink

Shape of the Week:

Decagon

Your Choice Book! | P is for Popcorn!

Give your child a paper plate bowl and a paint brush.

Have them use washable red paint to cover the outside of the plate.

Once the paint has dried have them glue cotton balls to the inside of the plate!

Tell them it's a bowl full of popcorn! | Homemade Snow Fun!

Mix 2 cups of hair conditioner with 4 cups of baking soda.

If the texture is too runny just add more baking soda to make it thicker.

Mix it all together to create some fun homemade snow!

Set out a plastic mat and have your child play with the pretend snow! | Hit Rudolph's Nose!

Using a poster paper: Draw a large Circle

Then draw a smaller circle in the middle!

Color the smaller circle red.

On either side of the red circle draw two eyes!

On the bottom draw a big smile!

Tape it securely onto a wall so that it is at your child's eye level! | Build Snowmen using mini marshmallows and toothpicks!

(Always supervise your child when working with small or pointy objects.) | P is for popcorn

-paper plate bowl.

-cotton balls

-red washable paint

-glue

-paint brush

Homemade Snow:

-plastic mat

-hair conditioner

-baking Soda

(Always supervise your child when playing with anything that they are not supposed to eat!) |

| | | | | Give your child some bean bags!

Have them do their best to hit Rudolph's Red nose from the middle of the room!! | | Hit Rudolph's nose

-poster paper

-tape

-black and red marker.

-bean bags

Build Marshmallow snowmen!

-toothpicks

-mini marshmallows

Always supervise your child when playing with small objects! |
| Tuesday | Letter of the Week: Pp

Number of the Week :16 | Macaroni shape art!

Use a black marker to draw a decagon on | Sensory Bin:

Mix some green food coloring with some water and | Busy Elf!

Have your child pretend that he/she is an elf. | Theme Puzzle!

Choose a child friendly | Macaroni Shape Art

-pink construction paper |

	Color of the Week: Pink Shape of the Week: Decagon Your Choice Book!	a sheet of pink construction paper! The shape should take up at least half of the page. Have your child count the sides! Next have them trace the lines with glue and then add dry elbow pasta for some macaroni shape art!	freeze it using 2 ice cube trays. Mix some red food coloring with some water and freeze it using 2 ice cube trays. Take the green and red cubes and place them in your sensory bin. Add some : -water -Scoops -plastic bowls	Their job is to sort the big toys from the small toys as fast as they can! In a basket place small and big stuffed toys. Place two empty containers on either side of the filled bin. Set the timer for 1 minute. Have your child sort the toys as fast as they can! Play some holiday music in the background!	holiday puzzle! Help your child put it together as you listen to some Christmas music!	-glue -dry elbow macaroni -marker Sensory Bin: Plastic Bin large enough to fit 3 pairs of shoes! -green and red ice cubes -water -plastic scoops -plastic bowl. Busy Elf! -3 large bins -big and small stuffed toys -timer -holiday music Christmas Theme Puzzle

						-Make sure it's age appropriate
Wednesday	Letter of the Week: Pp Number of the Week: 16 Color of the Week: Pink Shape of the Week: Decagon Your Choice Book!	Candy Cane Pattern! Using a piece of yellow construction paper draw a large letter P. It should take up at least half of the page. Have your child dip a finger in white paint and another in red paint! Have them trace the candy cane using their fingerprints in a red and white pattern!	Sensory Bin: Ball Pit! Place some palm size multicolor light weight plastic balls in your sensory bin! (The kind that you would find in a ball pit!) Have your child have fun identifying all of the different colors!	Shape Quest: Set the timer for 2 minutes. Have your child race around the house looking for the following shapes: circle square star: diamond rectangle triangle decagon-If you find this one make sure to take a picture! Follow your child with a paper where all the shapes are written	Snow Covered Tree! Choose a large pine cone! Have your child use washable green paint and a paint brush to cover the pine cone in green! Once the green paint has dried have them dip their brush in white washable paint to add on some snow marks!	Candy Cane Pattern! -yellow construction paper -washable red and white finger paint -marker Sensory Bin: plastic container big enough to fit 3 pairs of shoes! -multicolor plastic, light weight ball pit balls. Shape Quest: -piece of paper -marker/pen

				down! Every time they find a shape place a holiday themed sticker on the paper as a check mark for completion!		-holiday themed stickers -timer Snow Covered Tree! -large Pine Cone -washable Green Paint -washable White Paint -small paint brush
Thursday	Letter of the Week: Pp Number of the Week :16 Color of the Week: Pink Shape of the Week: Decagon Your Choice Book!	Silver Bells! Draw a large letter U on a piece of construction paper! It should take up at least half of the page! Turn the paper so that the U is upside down! Then draw a horizontal line to close the U! You should now	Guess the present! Have your child close their eyes! Set in front of them a stuffed toy, a plastic cup, a Christmas cookie, play dough, and a gift bow! Present the items one by one, and have your child feel them and	16 Energy Burn ! Have your child do - 16 jumping jacks -16 seconds of running in place 16 high knee kicks! 16 air squats! Make sure to play some dance music in the	Christmas Cards! Christmas Cards! You will need 3 blank greeting cards, and 3 envelopes. Ask your child to name 3 people that thy love, then ask them why they love	Silver Bells - construction Paper -washable Grey paint -child friendly paint brush -silver glitter -glue Always supervise your child when using glitter!

		have a Bell Shape! Have your child use washable grey paint to paint the inside of the bell! Once the paint has dried have them trace the bell with glue. Once they are done tracing. Sprinkle some silver glitter along the lines of the bell (You need to help them with this part to avoid a big sparkly mess!) Set it aside and let the glue dry. Once it is dry shake of the excess glitter into a container to discard.	then guess what they are!	background! Safety First! Make sure your child is comfortable doing the exercises and that they are hydrated. Modify as needed! Safety First!	each person. Write the name of the person and what the child says about them on the card. Give your 3 envelopes. Have them decorate their envelope with crayons, and Christmas stickers. Once they are done place each person's card in their own envelope give or mail to each individual.	-You can also buy glitter glue to avoid excess glitter! Guess the Present: --play dough -plastic cup -Christmas cookie -gift bow 16 Energy Burn -Dance Music! Christmas Cards: 3 Blank Cards 3 Envelopes Christmas Stickers -crayons -stamps if you are mailing them out

Friday	Letter of the Week: Pp	Nativity Scene Hand Print!	Sensory Bin: Number 16	Ice Box Push	Present Wrap	Nativity Scene Handprint!
	Number of the Week :16	Cover the inside of your child's hand in yellow washable paint!	Write the number 16 down on 16 different sticky notes! Place them in your sensory bin!	Fill a laundry basket with some rolled up white socks.	Give your child an empty shoe box, some wrapping paper, precut scotch tape, and some child friendly scissors!	-blue construction paper
	Color of the Week: Pink					-yellow washable paint (hay)
	Shape of the Week:	Have them place their hand in the center of a blue sheet of construction paper.	Next add some uncooked elbow pasta to your bin!	Using painter's tape create a zig zag line across the room.	Have them practice wrapping gifts!	-white washable paint (swaddling clothes)
	Decagon					
	Your Choice Book!		Have your child dig through the pasta to find the number 16!	Have your child push their ice box as fast as they can following the zig zag pattern!		-skin(your choice paint)
		When the yellow paint has dried.				-pencil
						-black marker
		Have use a small brush and washable white paint to draw and fill in an oval on the palm of the handprint.		When they get to the end of the line have them empty the basket and zig zag back!		Sensory Bin:16
						-large plastic bin big enough to fit 3 pairs of shoes
		Next have them dip their thumb in some skin color finger paint (your		Make sure to set the timer for 1 minute!		-dry elbow pasta
						-sticky notes
						-pen
						Always supervise

		choice color).

Gently leave their thumb print next to the white oval. The print should be touching the oval.

With a pencil draw some soft lines on the white oval. The white oval is the swaddling cloth.

Once the paint has dried , use a black marker to draw a happy face on the thumb print.

It's baby Jesus in the manger! | | | your child when playing with small objects that may pose choking hazard.

Ice Box Push

-rolled up white socks

-laundry basket

-painter's tape

-timer

Present Wrap

-wrapping paper enough to wrap a shoe box

-scotch tape

-child friendly scissors |

Artic Theme Week: 1

	Circle Time	Craft	Sensory	Gross Motor	Fine Motor	Materials Needed
Monday	Assessment week! Review Letters A-P Number:17 Color of the Week: Light Blue Shape of the Week: Cone Your Choice Book!	Polar Bear Craft! You will need a bowl and white chalk. You will also need a precut small black triangle for the nose(use construction paper) Using a white chalk and black construction paper as a base trace your chosen bowl to create a circle. That will be the face of the polar bear. Draw two mini circles for the ears.	Sensory Bin: Fill your bin with some blue Jell-O and some plastic scoops!	Iceberg Hop! Use regular white print paper Write down numbers 12-17. One number per paper. You could use half a sheet for each number as long as the number is big enough for child to see from a distance. Tape each sheet securely to the floor. Have the child hop from sheet to sheet as they say the number out loud! Ice Berg Hop!	Mini Snowball Count! Fill a bowl with mini marshmallows On a plastic/paper cup write the number 17. Have your child use some child friendly tweezers to transfer the mini marshmallows into the cup. Have them count the marshmallows as they transfer them.	Polar Bear Craft! -black construction paper -googly eyes -white washable paint -black marker -bowl -white chalk -paintbrush -Sensory Bin: -plastic bin big enough to fit 3 pairs of shoes -blue Jell-O (enough to fill the bottom of the bin! -plastic scoops (Always supervise

		Have your child use white washable paint and a paint brush to fill each circle. When the paint has dried have your child add two googly eyes. Have them glue the black triangle for the nose. Use a black marker to draw on a smile!				your child when playing with small objects or things that could potentially be swallowed.) Ice berg hop! -white paper -marker to write down number -tape Mini Marshmallow Count! -paper plate bowl -plastic/paper cup!
Tuesday	Assessment week! Review Letters A-P Number:17	Iceberg Craft! You will need a paper snow cone holder.	Sensory Bin: Fill your bin with some shaved ice, washable blue and a paint brush	Penguin Letter Splash! Place a large towel on the floor/plastic	Snowball Dot! Use a blue construction paper as your background.	Iceberg craft: -paper plate -paper snow cone holder.

	Color of the Week: Light Blue	Using white washable paint and a small paint brush have your child cover their cone!		mat on the floor.	Lay a white chalk on the paper and color back and forth until the paper is fully covered.	-washable blue and white paint
	Shape of the Week: Cone	Next have your child use blue washable paint to cover the inside of a paper plate.		On top of the towel place 3 plastic buckets/containers of water.	Next take a black marker and write the letter P in multiple places on the paper.	-small paintbrush -glue Sensory Bin: -plastic bin large enough to fit 3 pairs of shoes.
	Your Choice Book!	When the paint has dried on both items have them glue their cone on the plate!		On each bucket draw a letter. One letter per bucket! N, O, and P Have your child take turns throwing ping pong balls into each bucket.	Give your child a wet cotton ball and have them leave a mark on each of the letter P's.	-shaved ice enough to cover the bottom of the bin. -blue, and white washable paint. -paint brush
		Now you have an iceberg!		Have them identify the letter before tossing the balls. The balls will look like penguins going for a swim!		Penguin splash -3buckets/containers -water -large towel/mat -ping pong balls

						-washable marker to write down the letters. Always supervise your child when playing with water or small objects. Snowball Dot -blue Construction paper -cotton ball -white chalk -black marker
Wednesday	Assessment week! Review Letters A-P Number:17 Color of the Week: Light Blue Shape of the Week:	Artic Fox Face Using white construction paper, precut 2 triangles the size of your ring, middle, and index finger together. These will	Sensory Bin: Freeze some shaving cream in a plastic container. Break apart your frozen shaving cream and drop it in your	Icicle thrown: Cover some empty paper towel rolls in aluminum foil (3). Write down the number 17 on a piece of paper and	Shape Snow Flake! On a piece of blue/black construction paper draw a rectangle, square, hexagon, triangle, square	Artic Fox Face -blue Construction paper -white washable paint -black washable finger paint

	Cone Your Choice Book!	be your fox ears! Using a blue construction paper draw a horizontal oval. The oval should take up half of the sheet of paper. Next have your child dip a plastic white fork in washable paint. Have them stamp their fork in the oval until the oval is fully covered. When the paint is dried have your child glue on the two white triangles ears. Next have them dip their finger in some black	sensory bin (There should enough to fully cover the bottom). Add some artic themed plastic toys (penguins, polar bears etc.)	tape it to the wall. Have your child take aim and hit the number 17 with their icicle!	Have your child trace over them with glue Next cover the paper with some salt. Carefully shake the salt off over a sink. You will be left with snow shapes!	-plastic fork Sensory Bin: -plastic bin large enough to fit 3 pairs of shoes -frozen shaving cream -artic themed plastic toys (Always supervise your child when playing with small objects or anything that they are not supposed to eat.) Icicle Throw -3 empty paper towel rolls -aluminum Foil -regular paper print or lined paper

| | | washable finger paint and stamp it in the middle of the oval (That's the nose).

Next have them glue on some googly eyes! | | | | -tape

-marker

Shape Snow Flake:

- Constructio n paper blue /black

-salt

-glue

-marker |
|---|---|---|---|---|---|---|
| Thursday | Assessment week!

Review Letters A-P

Number:17

Color of the Week: Light Blue

Shape of the Week:

Cone

Your Choice Book! | Sea Lion Craft:

Precut a triangle the size of your pinky finger from a black piece of constructio n paper.

Have your child stuff a brown paper lunch bag with newspaper or magazines.

When they are done tie the opening with some yarn. | Sensory Bin:

Mix some blue food coloring with some water. Pour the mixture into 3-4 ice trays and freeze!

Once they are frozen drop them in your sensory bin. Add some water so your ice will float.

Add some plastic measuring cups. | Penguin Waddle

Fill a small bin with multiple color balloons. Place it next to your child.

Place an empty bin across the room.

Have your child place one balloon between their knees and waddle like a penguin across the room. Have | Bubble Wrap Blizzard!

Have your child use a paint brush to cover a piece of bubble wrap with white washable paint.

Have them flip the bubble wrap over and press it down on a blue piece of constructio n paper. | Sea Lion Craft:

-googly eyes

-paper lunch bag

- magazine/n ewspaper

-black constructio n paper triangle (for nose).

-glue

Sensory Bin:

-plastic Bin big enough to fit 3 pairs of shoes.

-water |

		Have them glue on some googly eyes to the bottom of the bag. Have them glue on a small black triangle nose.		them place the balloon in the empty bin and race back to the balloon bucket to grab another one. Have them do this until the bucket is empty. Make sure they identify the color of the balloon as they pick it up from the original bucket. Safety First! Make sure to clear the area of any tripping hazard, and that your child is comfortable completing the activity.	Once the paint dries have them add some drops of silver glitter glue! Have them lift up the paper to see their newly created blizzard picture!	-blue ice -plastic measuring cups Penguin Waddle: -2 empty bins -multiple color balloons (5) Bubble Wrap Blizzard -Paper sized bubble wrap sheet -white washable paint - small paint brush -silver glitter glue
Friday	Assessment week!	Draw a large number 17 on a piece	Sensory Bin: Fill your bin with:	Build an Igloo! Have your child use	Scissor Practice On a sheet of regular	Number Craft: - constructio

Review Letters A-P Number:17 Color of the Week: Light Blue Shape of the Week: Cone Your Choice Book!	of constructio n paper. The number should be at least half of the size of the paper. Have your child trace the number 17 with glue, and then have them add 17 mini marshmallo ws. Make sure to help them count! Once they have counted to 17 feel free to add more marshmallo ws and count even higher!	-water -bubble bath bubbles and some -plastic toy boats	couch and bed pillows to construct a play igloo!	paper draw a 2 horizontal lines and a 2 zig-zag lines across the page. Have your child practice using child friendly scissors.	n paper (any color) -mini marshmallo ws -glue Sensory Bin: -plastic bin large enough to fit 3 pairs of shoes -bubble bath bubbles -plastic toy boats -water Always supervise your child when playing with water! Build an Igloo! -couch and bed pillows Scissor Practice: -child friendly scissors

						-paper - marker/pen

Artic Theme Week: 2

	Circle time	Craft	Sensory	Gross Motor	Fine Motor	Materials needed
Monday	The letter of the week: Qq

Number of the Week :18

Color of the Week: Dark Blue

Shape of the Week:

Pyramid

Your Choice Book! | Q is for Queen

Use a construction paper

Draw a zig zag pattern across the center.

Now use a pair of scissors to cut the paper in half following the pattern.

Give half of the paper to your child.

Give them their choice of craft décor items to decorate the crown. Ex) crayons, sparkles, and buttons, glue, etc.

(Always supervise | Sensory Bin:

Fill your bin with the following:

-buttons

-plastic scoops | Light Blue/Dark Blue sort!

Place items that are dark blue and light blue items in one large plastic bin.

Example: scarf mittens plastic cup stuffed animals blanket

Set two empty bins on either side of the filled container.

Tape a dark blue construction paper to the side of one of the bins, and a light blue construction paper to | Dotting Numbers

On a piece of construction paper write down numbers 15 through 18 in multiple areas on the sheet (repeat each of the numbers at least 3 times).

Have your child use a yellow dotter to mark 15, a red dotter to mark 16, a purple to dot 17, and a blue dotter to mark 18. | Queen's Crown:

-yellow construction paper

-scissors

-glue

Child's choice: buttons, sparkles, colors crayons, etc.

Always supervise your child when working with small objects that may pose choking hazard.

Sensory Bin:

- plastic bin large enough to fit 3 pairs of shoes |

		your child when they are working with small objects). When they are done tape the ends of the crown together. It's the Queen's Crown!		the other bin. Have the child sort the items as fast as they can!		-mini buttons -plastic scoops Always supervise your child when working with small objects that may pose choking hazard. Dark Blue/ Light Blue Sort 3 large plastic bins 5 items that are light blue or have light blue on them ex) scarf, blanket, stuffed animal, plastic cup, shirt, pillow, etc. 5 items that are dark blue or have light blue on them ex) scarf, blanket,

					stuffed animal, plastic cup, shirt, pillow, etc. Dotting Numbers Red, Yellow, Blue, Purple washable paint dotters construction paper : white marker
Tuesday	The letter of the week: Qq Number of the Week: 18 Color of the Week: Dark Blue Shape of the Week: Pyramid Your Choice Book!	Moose Craft Using washable brown paint. Cover the bottom of your child's foot. Have them leave their footprint on a white construction paper. (The foot will be the	Sensory Bin: Mix some blue food coloring with some water and pour it in your bin! Add some shaving cream globs and some plastic toy penguins	Gross Motor: Winter Dress Up! Brrrrr! It's getting cold outside! Give your child a cap, coat, mittens, and boots! Set the timer for 1 minute!	Moose Antlers Build some moose antlers by bending and twisting together some brown pipe cleaners!	Moose Craft: -white construction paper -washable brown paint - googly eyes -paint brush Sensory Bin: -plastic container large

		head of the moose.) Next cover the inside of your child's hands with brown washable paint. Have them place their hands on either side of the footprint so that their thumbs touch the toe prints. (The hands are the antlers.) When the paint has dried have your child glue two googly eyes to their moose!		How fast can you put on your winter wear?		enough to fit 3 pairs of shoes. -plastic toy penguins -water -dark blue food coloring -shaving cream Winter Dress Up! -winter coat -cap -mittens -snow boots Moose Antlers - brown pipe cleaners
Wednesday	The letter of the week: Qq Number of the Week :18	Orca Craft! Have your child use a paint brush to completely cover one	Blue Pasta: Mixed some cooked pasta with some dark blue	Pyramid of Pillows! Have your child use different size pillows	Trace the Letter Qq Using broken dash lines draw the letter "Q q"	Orca Craft: -black and white washable paint

Color of the Week: Dark Blue Shape of the Week: Pyramid Your Choice Book!	side of a brown paper lunch bag using white washable paint. Have them paint the other side with black washable paint. When the paint has dried. Have your child stuff a brown paper bag with newspaper or magazines crumbled pages. When the bag is stuffed tie the end of it using a piece of yarn or twine. Have them glue on two googly eyes	washable paint! Place the painted pasta on a large white poster paper. Have your child have fun painting with pasta! Make sure to set a plastic mat beneath the work area.	to build a pyramid!	multiple times on a regular sheet of paper (10-15 times). Have your child use a blue crayon to practice tracing the letter!	-magazine or news paper -twine/ yarn -paint brush Blue Pasta Sensory Play -white poster paper. -dark blue washable paint -cooked spaghetti -mat Pyramid of Pillows! -pillows of small, medium, and large sizes Trace the letter Qq -regular sheet of print or lined paper

		to the sides of the bag!			-dark blue crayon
Thursday	The letter of the week: Qq Number of the Week: 18 Color of the Week: Dark Blue Shape of the Week: Pyramid Your Choice Book!	Shape Artic Hare! On a piece of blue construction paper. Draw a square in the middle the size of your palm this is the face of your snow hare! On the head of the hare add two long ovals these are the ears! In the middle of the square draw a small triangle this is the nose! Have your child dip their finger in some white washable paint to	Frozen Water Balloons! Fill up some water balloons! Put them in the freezer. Once they are frozen take the balloons out and drop them in your sensory bin. Make enough to fill the bottom of the bin!	What shape is it? Using white side walk chalk draw a large trapezoid, pentagon, octagon, and a rectangle on the ground. Give your child a bucket full of bean bags. Have them identify the shape before throwing the bean bag to hit their mark! If you are doing this activity in doors draw the shapes on a regular sheet of paper and then tape	Icicles Use a piece of dark blue construction paper as a base. Draw three large triangles. Turn the page so that the triangles are upside down like icicles. Have your child paint the inside of the icicles with white washable paint. When the paint is dry have them trace the outside with glue. Carefully sprinkle some white rice on the	Shape Artic Hare: -white and pink washable finger paint -blue construction paper -marker to draw shapes Sensory Bin: -plastic bin large enough to fit 3 pairs of shoes - frozen water balloons What shape is it? -bucket -bean bags -side walk chalk If you are indoors :

| | | trace the lines of the circle and ovals.

Next have them fill in the entire circle and oval with multiple finger prints so that it is completely covered!

Have them add two googly eyes

Finally have your child dip their finger in some pink washable finger paint and dot the nose!

Have your child identify each shape before they begin dotting! | | them to the ground! | glue and let it sit.

After the glue dries remove the excess rice over a container or sink to avoid messiness. | -4 regular sheets of paper

-marker

-tape

Icicles:

-dark blue construction paper

-white washable paint

-glue

-white rice

-paint brush

-marker

-water |
|---|---|---|---|---|---|---|
| Friday | The letter of the week: Qq | Snow Owl Craft! | Artic Sounds: | Carry the sea lion to safety! | Alphabet Review | Snowy Owl |

	Number of the Week :18	Precut a small triangle using orange construction paper. This is the owl beak. Precut two small circles from a yellow construction paper, and dot the middle of each circle with a marker. These are the owl eyes. Using a black marker trace a bowl onto a sheet of blue construction paper to create a circle. The circle should be at least half of the page.	Have your child listen to some Artic Sounds: -ice breaking -owl hooting -walrus bark -orca calls	Fill a large bin with small pillows (At least 5). Play a game of pretend sea lion rescue! Tell your child that they have to rescue the sea lions from the hungry whale. Have your child them carry the small pillows (sea lions) as fast as they can across the room and drop them in an empty container. Only one sea lion at a time! Set the timer for 1 minute	Write down letters Aa-Qq Have your child identify each letter. Have them glue a dry bean to each letter that they have mastered.	-white washable paint -blue construction paper -orange construction paper -yellow print paper -marker -white store bought feathers -glue Artic Sounds Recorded sounds of: -ice breaking -owl hooting -walrus bark -orca calls Sea Lion Rescue! -2 empty bins -5 small pillows or

Color of the

Week: Dark Blue

Shape of the Week:

Pyramid

Your Choice Book!

		Use white washable paint to cover the inside of your child's hands. Have them leave their handprints on either side of the circle. These are your owl wings. Have your child glue on the two owl eyes, and the beak. Have them glue the white feathers to cover the rest of the area in the circle.				stuffed animals -timer: modify time as needed Alphabet Review: -white construction paper -dry beans -glue -marker

Artic Theme Week: 3

	Circle Time	Craft	Sensory	Gross Motor	Fine Motor	Materials Needed
Monday	The letter of the week: Rr Number of the Week: 19 Color of the Week: Dark Green Shape of the Week: Cylinder Your Choice Book!	R is for Rainbow! Have your child use a sheet of white construction paper, a paint brush, and washable paint to create a beautiful rainbow! Use the following colors: green blue red pink, yellow purple Have them identify each colors as they are creating their art!	ABC Soup Sensory Bin: Fill your container up with water, Add some drops of green food coloring, Add plastic bowls, and plastic ABC letters	Skip to 19 Have your child skip across the room while counting to 19!	Build a Cabin Help your child build a cabin with glue and popsicle sticks.	R is for Rainbow -washable paint :red, green, purple, blue, yellow, pink -white construction paper -paint brush ABC Soup -Plastic Container big enough to fit 3 pairs of shoes -water -green food coloring -ABC plastic letters -plastic bowls (Always supervise your child when playing with water or

						small objects that may pose choking hazard). Skip to 19 No materials needed Build A Cabin -Glue -popsicle sticks.
Tuesday	The letter of the week: Rr Number of the Week :19 Color of the Week: Dark Green Shape of the Week: Cylinder Your Choice Book!	ABC Snowballs On a blue piece of construction paper. Write down letters A –R Have your child identify each letter. Have them glue on a cotton ball to all of the letters that they have mastered.	Sensory Bin: Fill your bin with the following - dry green peas -plastic funnels	Shape Hop! Using a green piece of side walk chalk. Draw the following shapes: pentagon octagon triangle trapezoid Space them enough so that your child has room to hop from	Letter Writing: Fill a plastic tray or paper plate with salt. Add some green Kool aide powder. Have your child practice writing their letters on the tray with their fingers.	ABC snowballs -blue construction paper -cotton balls -marker to draw on letters -glue Sensory Bin: -plastic Container large enough to fit 3 pairs of shoes

				one shape to the next. Have them identify each shape before they hop over!		-dry green peas -plastic funnels Always supervise your child when playing with small objects that may pose choking hazard). Shape Hop: -green side walk chalk -If you are indoors use painter's tape to create the shapes or draw them on a different pieces of regular print paper and tape them securely to the floor. Letter Writing:

					-plastic tray/paper plate -salt -green Kool aide powder
Wednesday	The letter of the week: Rr Number of the Week: 19 Color of the Week: Dark Green Shape of the Week: Cylinder Your Choice Book!	Colorful Cylinder Craft! You will need an empty toilet roll! Precut two circles the size of the openings of the toilet roll! Cover the openings of the roll with a piece of construction paper so that it forms a closed cylinder. Glue or tape the paper securely to the roll. Have your child use washable paint (their | Sensory Bin: Fill your sensory bin with some uncooked green veggies ex) green beans, green zucchini, snap peas!	Sack Catch! Give your child a large pillow case. Have them stand across the room. Tell them that they are to catch as many balls as they can with their sack. Make sure to use soft balls or some soft rolled up socks. Take turns throwing and catching with your child!	Creative Art: Give your child some googly eyes, paper, yarn, glue a paper plate, and some crayons, Have them build a craft all on their own.	Colorful Cylinder: washable paint -paint brush -construction paper -glue Green Veggie Bin: Plastic bin large enough to fit 3 pairs of shoes -green veggies ex) uncooked green beans, snap peas. Zucchini etc. Always supervise your child when

		choice colors) to decorate their cylinder.				working with things they could potentially ingest or may pose choking hazard! Creative Art: -yarn -googly eyes -glue -yarn -paper plate -crayons
Thursday	The letter of the week: Rr Number of the Week :19 Color of the Week: Dark Green Shape of the Week: Cylinder Your Choice Book!	Shape Walrus Using a piece of brown construction paper cut a large circle. It should be at least half the size of the paper. Next cut a trapezoid to be used as the walrus tail. It should be	Sensory Bin Fill your bin with the following: -water -rocks -leaves -twigs -plastic scoops	Yarn Obstacle course! Unravel Yarn across a room to create an obstacle course! (Think zig zagging Spider web). Have your child climb over and under the yarn to get	Marshmallow Snowflakes Give your child a plastic bowl full of mini marshmallows. Also provide them with some tooth pics. Help them to create some marshmallo	Shape Walrus: -brown, white construction paper -googly eyes -glue Sensory Bin: -plastic bin large enough to fit 3 pairs of shoes. -rocks -water

		about the size of your hand.		to the other side!	w snowflakes!	-leaves
						-twigs
		-Using a white construction paper cut two rectangles (tusks). Should be about the size of your middle and index fingers together.				(Always supervise your child when playing with water or small objects that may pose choking hazard)
						Yarn Obstacle course
		Help your put together and glue all the pieces to form a walrus.				-Yarn
						-tape is always helpful
		Add two googly eyes!				Marshmallow snowflakes
						-toothpicks
						-mini marshmallows
						(Always supervise your child when working with small objects that may pose

						choking hazard.)
Friday	The letter of the week: Rr Number of the Week :19 Color of the Week: Dark Green Shape of the Week: Cylinder Your Choice Book!	Snow Storm Craft! On a piece of black construction paper create a snow storm! Have your child dip a dry sponge into white washable paint. Have them stamp their sponge throughout	Sensory Bin: Fill your bin with the following: -dry white rice and -plastic funnels	Using sidewalk chalk create 6 large squares Write down numbers 14-19 (one number per square). Space them out far enough to allow your child to hop from number to number! Have your child hop to	Color Sort Have your child color sort Legos blocks. Colors: -red -blue -green -yellow	Snow Storm -black construction paper -sponge -white washable paint -glitter glue (silver) Sensory Bin: Plastic bin large enough to fit 3 pairs of shoes.

		the paper to create a picture of a snow storm! When the paint has dried have them add some silver glitter glue drops for shimmer!		each number. Make sure they identify each of the numbers as they hop to them.		-un cooked rice -funnels Number Hop -Side Walk Chalk -If you are indoors use painter's tape to create squares. Write down the numbers on a regular sized paper and tape them down securely. Color Sort: Lego blocks: -red -blue -green -yellow

Artic Theme Week: 4

	Circle Time	Craft	Sensory Bag	Gross Motor	Fine Motor	Materials Needed
Monday	The letter of the week: Ss Number of the Week :20 Color of the Week: White Shape of the Week: Arrow Your Choice Book!	S is for Snowman Using a blue construction paper draw 3 circles one on top of the other. They should each be about the size of your hand. Have your child use white washable paint to color in each circle. Next have them use a thin small brush to draw on the nose with orange paint. Then have them use a thin small brush and black	Fill a Ziploc bag with clear hair gel and some silver glitter Place a black construction paper on the table, then place the bag on top. Make sure it is completely sealed and tape it down. Have your child squish to bag to create a silver storm!	Javelin Throw Stuff a bean bag inside an empty paper towel roll to give it some weight. Have your child throw their javelin. Using a piece of painter's tape mark down how far they were able to throw it! Make sure to cheer them on!	Arrow Shapes On a regular sheet of print/lined paper draw a large arrow. It should take up most of the paper. Have your child trace the arrow shape using play dough.	S is for snowman -blue construction paper -white/black/orange washable paint -paint brushes -Silver Storm -Ziploc bag -silver glitter -clear hair gel -black construction paper Javelin Throw -Empty paper towel roll -bean bag

159

		washable paint to dot 2 black eyes. Finally, have them dip their fingers in white finger paint and dot around the snowman to create snow!				Arrow Shapes -Play dough -paper -marker to draw shape
Tuesday	The letter of the week: Ss Number of the Week: 20 Color of the Week: White Shape of the Week: Arrow Your Choice Book!	Snow Monster Craft -using red construction paper precut a small rectangle the size of your pinky finger. Have your child glue white cotton balls onto a water bottle. Have them cover the bottle completely.	Sensory Bin Fill your bin with the following: -dry white beans -plastic measuring cups	Number Run! Using Side walk Chalk write down numbers 1-20 on the ground. Have your child race through the number line as they count out loud!	Using a regular sheet of print/lined paper as a base, use a pen/marker to draw the letter "S" (At least 10 times) using broken lines ------ Have your child use their favorite color to trace the letter "S".	Snow Monster Craft cotton Balls water Bottle -red construction paper/red print paper -googly eyes Glue Sensory Bin: -plastic bin large enough to fit 3 pairs of shoes -dry white beans

		Have them glue on two googly eyes. Have them glue on a small red rectangle (the mouth)				-plastic measuring cups Number Line Run! -side walk chalk If you are indoors use painter's tape to create the number line. Use two or three long pieces so that you can make it thick enough to write down the numbers big enough for your child to see them! Trace "S" -print/lined paper -crayons - marker/pen

| Wednesday | The letter of the week: Ss

Number of the Week: 20

Color of the Week: White

Shape of the Week: Arrow

Your Choice Book! | Decorate your Arrow Craft!

Using a piece of blue construction paper and a black marker. Draw 4 large arrows. They should take up the full page.

Have your child tear small pieces of white tissue paper.

Have them glue on their pieces of tissue paper onto their arrows. | Sensory Bin:

Fill you sensory bin with the following:

-dry lima beans

-plastic toy trucks/snow plows | Snowball Shotput throw!

Give your child a pair of socks

Have them spin around and let their snowball fly as far as they can!

Make sure your mark how far their snowball has flown using painter's tape. | Geometric shape tiles

Have your child build various designs using shape tiles! | Decorate your Arrow Craft!

-construction paper blue

-white tissue paper

-marker to draw arrows

Sensory Bin:

-plastic bin large enough to fit 3 pairs of shoes

-dry lima beans

-plastic toy trucks (snow plows)

Snowball Shotput

-rolled up white socks

-painter's tape

Geometric Shape Designs |

| | | | | | | Geometric tiles

Always supervise your child when working with small objects that may pose choking hazard. |
|---|---|---|---|---|---|---|
| Thursday | The letter of the week: Ss

Number of the Week :20

Color of the Week: White

Shape of the Week: Arrow

Your Choice Book! | Sparkly Arrows!

On a piece of white construction paper use a black marker to draw 4 large arrows. They should take the full page.

Have your child paint each of the arrows using washable paint. Have them choose different colors. | Pouring Station

Fill your bin with the following:

-water

-plastic funnels

-plastic sized drinking cups | Pillow Hop!

Lay 5 small pillows on the ground.

Leave enough space between so your child can easily hop over them!

Tell your child that they are to hop like an artic hare over each of the pillows! | Build a Dog Sled!

Use a small piece of card board.

Glue 5 popsicle sticks onto the cardboard. They are to be laying down flat.

Glue two strips of aluminum foil on the bottom of the sled to help it cut through the ice! | Sparkly Arrows!

-white construction paper

-paint brush

-washable paint

-black marker

-glitter glue

Sensory Bin: Pouring Station

-plastic bin large enough to fit 3 pairs of shoes

-different sized plastic |

		When the paint dries have them trace their arrows once more with some glitter glue!				drinking cups Pillow Hop! -5 small pillows Build a Dog Sled 5 popsicle sticks Small cardboard big enough so that the 5 popsicle sticks can easily be glued together on their flat side. 2 strips of aluminum foil Glue
Friday	The letter of the week: Ss Number of the Week: 20	ABC Snowballs! Using a black pen write down letters A-S on a regular	How does it Feel? Warm up a towel in the microwave touch it to make sure it's' not hot	Create 4 large squares on the floor using side walk chalk. On the first square	Match the Numbers Fold a black construction paper in half so that it forms 2 columns.	ABC snow balls! -regular sheet of paper -glue

Color of the Week: White Shape of the Week: Arrow Your Choice Book!	sheet of paper. Have your child Identify each letter. As they identify each letter have glue on a fuzzy white cotton ball!	before you give it to your child! -chill a bottle of water in the fridge. Have your child close their eyes and feel the water bottle. Have them describe the temperature And texture. Do the same for the towel.	write down your child's name. In the second square write the number 20. In the third square write down the letter S, and in the fourth square draw an arrow. Have your child take their bounciest ball and identify what is in each of the squares before bouncing their ball off of each square!	On each column write down the number 17,18, 19, and 20 in the following form: 17 17 18 19 19 20 20 18 Note: Use white chalk to write down the numbers. Have the child take the white chalk and match the numbers by drawing a connecting line between the matching numbers.	-cotton balls -black pen/marker How does it Feel? -cold water bottle -warm towel 4 Square Bounce -bouncy ball -side walk chalk If you are working indoors use painter's tape to create the squares and write down the material on a regular sheets of print/lined paper and tape them securely to the floor. Match the Numbers

						-black construction paper -white chalk

Valentine's Day Theme Week: 1

	Circle Time	Craft	Sensory	Gross Motor	Fine Motor	Materials Needed
Monday	The letter of the week: Tt

Number of the Week :21

Color of the Week: Red

Shape of the Week: Heart

Your Choice Book! | T is for Turtle Craft!

Give your child a paper plate bowl.

Have your child decorate their turtle shell with some precut red construction paper hearts, and some red glitter glue! | Sensory Bin

Fill your bin with the following:

-dry red beans

-plastic measuring cups | Red Balloon Tennis!

Play a game of tennis with your child using a red balloons! | Red cookies!

Give your child some fun red play dough, plastic play rolling pin, and some plastic cookie cutters! | T is for Turtle Craft!

-paper plate bowl

-red construction paper

-red glitter glue

Sensory Bin:

-plastic Bin large enough to fit 3 pairs of shoes

-dry red beans

-plastic measuring cups

(Always supervise your child when playing with small objects that may pose choking hazard.) |

						Red Balloon Tennis! -red balloons! Blow up 3 balloons just in case one or two pop! -child tennis racket Red Cookies: -red play dough -child friendly cookie cutters -plastic child friendly rolling pin
Tuesday	The letter of the week: Tt Number of the Week:21 Color of the Week: Red Shape of the Week:	Heart Craft! Using a black marker, draw a large heart on a piece of white construction paper. The shape should take	Sensory Bin Fill your bin with the following: -dry pasta shells -different sized plastic bowls	Hearts and Number Hop! Using red construction paper and a pair of scissors cut out 7 hearts about the size of your two hands!	Heart Stickers! Fold a regular sheet of print/lined paper so that when it opens it has 6 squares. In the first square	Heart Craft: -red dotter -white construction paper -red glitter glue Sensory Bin:

	Heart Your Choice Book!	up most of the page. Have your child use a red dotter to cover the inside area of the heart. When the paint has dried have them trace the outside of the heart with some red glitter glue.		Using a black marker write down numbers 15-21. One on each heart. Tape the hearts down to the floor. Have your child identify each number as they hop from heart to heart.	write down your child's first name. In the second write the number 21. In the third square write down the letter "Tt". In the fourth square draw a heart shape. In the fifth square draw an arrow shape. In the sixth square write the letter "Ss". Have your child identify each one. As they identify the contents of each box have them add a heart sticker!	-plastic bin large enough to fit 3 pairs of shoes -dry shell pasta -plastic different sized bowls Heart and Number Hop -red constructio n paper -tape -scissors -marker Heart Stickers! -regular sheet of print/ lined paper -heart stickers

| Wednesday | The letter of the week: Tt

Number of the Week 21

Color of the Week: Red

Shape of the Week: Heart

Your Choice Book! | Hand Print Craft!

Paint the inside of your child's hand with red washable paint.

Have them place their hand on the center of a white piece of construction paper.

When the paint dries help them to trace their handprint with some silver glitter glue. | Sensory Bin:

Fill your bin with the following:

-red dry rice

-plastic funnels

Red Rice Instructions:

Fill a large Ziploc bag with some dry rice. Add some drops of red washable paint.

Seal the bag and move the contents around until the rice is fully covered in paint. Then set them out to dry on a mat.

When the paint is dry add the rice to the sensory bin! | Shape Splat!

Fill up some red balloons with water. Place them in a bucket next to your child.

Using side walk chalk draw a heart, oval, rectangle, and hexagon shape on the ground.

Have your child toss their balloon on each shape after they have identified them! | Heart Lacing!

Using a red poster board cut out a heart shape.

Use a hole puncher to punch holes along the edge of the shape.

Give your child some white yarn and have them lace the shape! | Hand print Craft!

-white construction paper

-red washable paint

-silver glitter glue

Sensory Bin:

-plastic bin large enough to fit 3 pairs of shoes

-plastic funnel

-red dyed uncooked rice

Shape Splat

-red balloons

-water

-bucket

-side walk chalk

If you are doing this activity |
|---|---|---|---|---|---|

						indoors use red socks instead of balloons and draw the shapes on regular sheets of paper. Heart Lacing -red poster paper -scissors -white yarn
Thursday	The letter of the week: Tt Number of the Week: 21 Color of the Week: Red Shape of the Week: Heart Your Choice Book!	Friendship Card Have your child tear up some red tissue paper Fold a pink constructio n paper in half. On the front flap draw a heart. Have your child cover the inside area of the heart with their red tissue paper.	Sensory Bin: Fill your bin with the following: - fruit loops and -plastic measuring cups	Big Bouncy Ball Catch! Play a game of catch with a big bouncy ball! Sing your ABC's as you take turns tossing and catching the ball!	Decorate with 21 Fuzzies! Use a pen/marker to draw the number 21 on a regular sheet of print/lined paper. It should take up at least half of the page. Have your child use glue and tweezers to decorate the number	Friendship Card -pink constructio n paper -red tissue paper -marker to write down message Sensory Bin -plastic Bin big enough to fit 3 pairs of shoes. -Fruit Loops -plastic measuring cups.

		On the inside of the card write down the words "I love you!" Have your child give the card to a friend of their choice!			with fuzzy pom poms	Big Bouncy Ball Catch -Big Bouncy Ball Decorate with 21 Fuzzies -Regular sheet of print/lined paper -fuzzy pom poms -glue -child friendly tweezers -marker/pen
Friday	The letter of the week: Tt Number of the Week:21 Color of the Week: Red Shape of the Week: Heart Your Choice Book!	Happy Heart Craft! Using a piece of red construction paper cut out a heart the size of your hand. Have your child glue on two googly eyes. Have them use a black	Sensory Bin Fill your bin with the following: -rigatoni pasta -plastic Bowels -plastic large spoon	Hand Ball! Play a fun game of hand ball with your child! Use a big bouncy ball to make it easier for your child to play!	Tracing Activity! Fold a regular sheet of paper so that it has 6 squares. Draw the following using broken lines --------	Happy Heart Craft! -red construction paper -white paper doily -glue -googly eyes Sensory Bin: -plastic bin large enough to

		marker to draw on a happy smile! Have them glue their heart onto a paper doily!			On the first square draw a heart, In the second square write the number 21. In the third write the letter "Tt" In the fourth draw a rectangle The Fifth write down the number 20. The sixth write down your child's name. Have your child identify each box and then use their favorite crayon to trace the number, word, shape or letter.	fit 3 pairs of shoes -dry rigatoni pasta -plastic Bowls -plastic Large Spoon Hand Ball! -Big Bouncy ball -wall Tracing Activity! -regular sheet of print/lined paper -crayons

Valentine's Day theme Week: 2

	Circle Time	Craft	Sensory	Gross Motor	Fine Motor	Materials Needed
Monday	The letter of the week: Uu

Number of the Week :22

Color of the Week: Peach

Shape of the Week: Cross

Your Choice Book! | "U" is for Umbrella

Using water colors and a small brush have your child decorate a coffee filter.

Once the filter had dried fold it in half and glue it onto a pipe cleaner.

Bend the bottom part of the pipe cleaner so that it looks like an umbrella handle (J) | Color Mixing

Fill a Ziploc bag with some shaving cream, a few drops of orange paint, and a few drops of white paint.

Make sure to seal it before giving it to your child.

Have your child squish the bag so that the colors mix. | Shape Fun!

On a regular sheets of paper draw the following shapes:

cross, oval, square, and a rectangle.

One shape per sheet.

Tape the sheets onto empty bins.

Give your child a container of ping pong balls.

Have them identify each shape as they attempt to land their ball in each of the containers. | Bean Count

Using a black marker/pen write down numbers 1-22 on a sheet of construction paper.

Give your child a cup of uncooked lima beans.

Have them count 22 lima beans and they glue them onto each of the numbers. | Umbrella Craft

-coffee Filter

-water Colors

-small Brush

-pipe Cleaner

-glue

Color Mixing

-orange and white washable paint

-shaving cream

-Ziploc bag

Shape Fun!

-4 empty plastic containers |

						-ping pong balls -regular sheets of paper -tape -marker/pen to draw shapes Bean Count -Lima Beans -plastic cup -glue -constructio n paper (any color) -marker/pen to write down numbers
Tuesday	The letter of the week: Uu Number of the Week:22 Color of the	Cross Street Shape Craft! Use a white piece of chalk to draw a large cross shape on a piece of black constructio	Sensory Bin Fill your bin with the following: -shredded paper	Ring Toss Grab some colorful rings and a play plastic cone! Set them outside and have your	Play Dough Trace Activity! Draw a large number 22 on a regular sheet of paper.	Cross Street Shape Craft! -black, red, yellow, blue constructio n paper -white chalk -glue

	Week: Peach Shape of the Week: Cross Your Choice Book!	n paper. The shape should take up the paper. Draw a cross inside the cross shape using broken lines ------------ Using red/yellow/ blue constructio n paper cut out: 4 rectangles 4squares, 8 circles (Help your child put together and glue on some shape cars on your cross street!		child identify the color of the ring as it is being tossed onto the cone!	Have your child trace the number using play dough	-scissors Sensory Bin: -plastic bin large enough to fit 3 pairs of shoes -shredded paper -Ring Toss: -Rings (hula hoop). If you don't have multiple hoops but still want to review colors just tape some colorful paper to their cone. -Cones (if you don't have cones you can just set out an empty coffee can as their mark. Trace 22 -play dough

Wednesday	The letter of the week: Uu Number of the Week :22 Color of the Week: Peach Shape of the Week: Cross Your Choice Book!	Peach Color Mix Using a black marker, draw a Large circle on a piece of white construction paper. Add a few drops of white and orange washable paint to the center. Have your child mix the colors using a paint brush so that the new color is peach! Have them cover the inside area of the circle with their mixed color. Then, using washable green paint, have them add some	Colorful dry pasta Fill 2 large Ziploc bags with some dry pasta Add some washable paint drops (Your choice of color) to each bag. Shake them so that the contents are fully covered in paint, then set them aside to dry on a plastic mat. Once it is dry pour the painted pasta into your sensory bin!	Letter Wall Balls! Using a black marker, write down the letters "Ss", "Tt", and "Uu" on separate sheets of paper! Tape them to the wall. Give your child a bouncy ball! Have them identify each letter as they bounce the ball of the wall!	Shape Review Fold a regular sheet of paper so that when it opens up it has 6 squares. Using a black marker draw the following shapes One shape per box cross hexagon rectangle triangle circle oval square Have your child take their favorite color washable marker and circle each	Peach Color Mix -washable orange, white, and green paint -white construction paper -black marker Sensory Bin: -dry pasta -washable paint -Ziploc -plastic mat -sensory bin: plastic bin large enough to fit 3 pairs of shoes Always supervise your child when playing with small objects that could pose choking hazard.

		green leaves to their peach!			one as they identify them.	Letter Wall balls! -3 regular sheets of paper -marker -tape -bouncy ball Shape Review -black Pen/Marker to draw shapes -regular sheet of paper -washable marker
Thursday	The letter of the week: Uu Number of the Week :22 Color of the Week: Peach Shape of the Week: Cross	Friendship Card Craft! Fold a piece of red construction paper in half. On the front flap of the card draw a heart. Have your child dip their fingers into some white	Rain Bow Rice Fill 3 Ziploc bags with some dry rice Add some washable paint (Your choice of colors). Make sure each bag has a	ABC and Number Challenge! Have your child lunge across the room When they get to the end have them sing their ABCs Have them Hop back across the	Magnet Fun! Have your child build with magnet tiles!	Friendship Card Craft! -red construction paper -white washable finger-paint -glue -dry pasta shells -black marker/pen

| | Your Choice Book! | washable finger paint. Have them fill the inside area of the heart with their prints.

When the paint is dried have them trace the outside with glue. Have them add some dry pasta shells.

Once the front flap has dried:

Have your child choose a friend.

Ask them 3 reasons why they love spending time with this person.

Write down their answers inside the card.

Give this card to their | different color.

Shake it so that the contents of each bag are fully covered, then spread the contents out to dry on a plastic mat.

Once the rice is dry pour it into your sensory bin.

Add some plastic funnels! | room. When they get there have them count 1-22!

Make sure give them a sticker and a high five when they complete their challenge!

Safety First! Make sure your child is comfortable completing the exercises and that they stay hydrated. Modify or change as needed. | | Sensory Bin:

-plastic bin big enough to fit 3 pairs of shoes.

-plastic funnels

-washable paint

-Ziploc bags

-plastic mat

-dry rice

ABC and Number Challenge!

-prize stickers

Magnet Fun!

-magnet play tiles |
|---|---|---|---|---|---|

		chosen friend.				
Friday	The letter of the week: Uu Number of the Week :22 Color of the Week: Peach Shape of the Week: Cross Your Choice Book!	Valentine's Day Card Collection Box Give your child a shoe box and some red washable paint. Have them paint the outside of the shoe box. Have them tear pink tissue paper and glue the pieces to the lid of the box. Make it so that the lid is fully covered Finally, have them dip their finger in some pink finger-paint and dot the box!	What fruit is it? Have your child close their eyes! Give your child a peach, banana, and an orange! Have them feel and smell each fruit. Have them guess what type of fruit it is.	Shapes and Water balloons! Using side walk chalk. Draw a trapezoid, cross, heart, and a circle on the ground. Give your child some water balloons! Have them identify each shape and then aim and pop their balloon on the correct shape!	Counting with blocks! On 3 note cards write down the numbers 10, 15, and 21. One number per card. Use counting blocks to build towers with the number of blocks that matches the card.	Valentine's Card Collection Box -shoe Box -pink finger-paint -pink tissue paper -red washable paint -paint brush Fruit Guess -anana -orange -peach Shapes and Water balloons! -water balloons -sidewalk chalk (If you are working indoors use rolled up socks or

						bean bags instead of balloons. Draw shapes on regular print/lined paper and tape them to the ground)
						Counting with blocks!
						-counting blocks
						-notecards
						-marker to write numbers on card

Valentines Theme Week: 3

	Circle Time	Craft	Sensory	Gross Motor	Fine Motor	Materials Needed
Monday	The letter of the week: Vv

Number of the Week :23

Color of the Week: Brown

Shape of the Week: Sphere

Your Choice Book! | V is for Vase Craft!

Give your child a paint brush and some purple washable paint. Have your child fully paint the outside of plastic/paper cup.

Next, have them dip their finger in some white washable finger paint and dot the vase!

Place some fresh flowers in their vase! | Fill a Ziploc bag with some shaving cream, add some drops of washable red paint, and some drops of washable orange paint.

Make sure that it is sealed. Tape the bag to the table and have your child use their fingers to mix the paints together to create a new color! | Kick the Spheres!

Line up some kick balls!

Space them out!

Have your child run to each ball and kick it as hard as they can!

Make sure to cheer them on!

Kick that sphere as hard as you can! | Number Trace

Write the number 23 on a regular sheet of paper. It should take up at least half of the paper.

Have your child trace the number 23 with some fun stickers! | V is for Vase

-plastic cup
-purple and white washable paint
-paintbrush
-fresh flowers that are small enough to fit in the cup

Paint Mixing! Ziploc Bag
-washable red and orange Paint

Kick the Spheres

-kick balls

Number Trace
-print/lined paper
-marker/pen to draw number
-fun stickers (cartoons, hearts, happy faces, etc.) |

Tuesday	The letter of the week: Vv	Painting Spheres	Sensory Bin	Pop the Spheres!	Alphabet Review	Painting Spheres
		Give your child a Styrofoam ball.	Fill your bin with the following:	Blow some bubbles and have your child pop as many	Write letters "Oo" through "Vv"	-Styrofoam ball -washable paints -paint brush
	Number of the Week:23		-dry brown Rice		On a regular sheet of print/lined paper.	Sensory Bin:
	Color of the Week: Brown	Have them use washable paint and a paint brush to decorate their ball with their choice of colors!	-plastic scoops and funnels	bubbles as they can before they hit the ground!		-plastic bin large enough to fit 3 pairs of shoes
	Shape of the Week: Sphere				Have your child identify each letter!	-dry brown rice -plastic Scoops -plastic Funnels
	Your Choice Book!				Have them add a sticker to each letter that they	Pop the Spheres!

					identify correctly.	-bubbles! Alphabet Review -stickers -regular sheet of print/lined paper -pen to write down the letters.
Wednesday	The letter of the week: Vv Number of the Week :23 Color of the Week: Brown Shape of the Week: Sphere Your Choice Book!	People that we love! Using a poster board and printed photos create a beautiful collage of the people that your child love! Make sure these are extra copies. You do not want you accidentally tear your only copy. Glue or tape the photographs onto a poster board! -	Sensory Bin Fill your Bin with the following: -chocolate rice cereal -plastic scoops -plastic funnels -plastic bowels	Neighborhood Shapes! On a regular sheet of print/lined paper, draw a square, rectangle, triangle, circle, oval, and octagon. Give the paper to your child along with a crayon and a clip board! Go for a walk around the neighborhood together. Have them look for the shapes and mark them off as they go!	Sorting Colors! Place a yellow, red, green and blue pieces of construction paper on the table. Give your child some matching color poms poms. Have them place the pomp oms on their matching paper	People that we love! -printed copies of photos of loved ones! -glue/tape -poster paper Sensory Bin: -plastic bin large enough to fit 3 pairs of shoes -chocolate rice cereal -plastic funnels -plastic bowls Neighborhood Shapes -regular sheet of paper -clipboard -crayon - marker/pen

						to draw shapes Sorting Colors: -Colorful pom poms (same color as the construction paper). -blue, red, green, yellow construction paper
Thursday	The letter of the week: Vv Number of the Week :23 Color of the Week: Brown Shape of the Week: Sphere Your Choice Book!	Red and White Pattern On a piece of pink construction paper use a black marker draw number 23. It should be at least half of the size of the paper. Have your child dip their finger in some red and white washable finger paint. Have them trace the number with their	Sensory Bin: Spheres! Fill your bin with some hand sized bouncy or plastic balls!	Knock Down the Tower! Create a pyramid of paper/plastic cups. Give your child a hand sized ball and see how many cups they can knock down!	Free Paint! Give your child a piece of white construction paper, paintbrush and some water colors!	Red and White Pattern -pink construction paper -red and white washable finger paint -black marker Sensory Bin: -plastic bin large enough to fit 3 pairs of shoes -hand sized bouncy balls or plastic Knock Down the Tower -plastic cups -child friendly

		finger prints. Create a red and white pattern. Ask them what color should go next as they dot the number!				hand sized ball Free Paint -white construction paper -water colors
Friday	The letter of the week: Vv Number of the Week :23 Color of the Week: Brown Shape of the Week: Sphere Your Choice Book!	Bouquet of Flowers! Give your child a piece of pink construction paper Give them a carnation flower. Have them dip their flower in some red, purple and white washable paint! Have them gently stamp their flower around their paper.	Sensory Bin: Gardening Theme Fill your bin with the following: -clean dirt - pebbles - wild flowers -plastic shovels.	Soccer Training! Line up 10 plastic cups! Make sure to space them out to give your child room to maneuver their ball around them! Cheer them on as they make their way around the cups in a zig zag fashion!	Salt and Coco powder Tray Activity! Fill a paper plate or plastic tray with some salt and coco powder. Make sure to place a plastic mat beneath the work area to avoid added clean up! Have your child practice writing numbers 1-23 on their tray!	Bouquet of Flowers Craft: -carnation flower -red, white, and purple washable paint -pink construction paper Salt and Coco tray Activity: -paper plate or plastic tray -salt and coco powder Sensory Bin: Gardening -plastic bin large enough to fit 3 pairs of shoes

						-clean dirt -wild flowers -pebbles -plastic shovels Always supervise your child when working with small items that may pose choking hazard. Soccer Training -10 plastic Cups or cones if you have them! - child sized soccer ball

Valentine's Day Theme Week: 4

	Circle Time	Craft	Sensory	Gross Motor	Fine Motor	Materials Needed
Monday	The letter of the week: Ww Number of the Week :24 Color of the Week: Green (Color Mixing) Shape of the Week: Cube Your Choice Book!	W is for Whale Craft! Using black construction paper precut a triangle (the size of your hand). Give your child a paper plate. Have them use black washable paint to cover the top half of the plate, and white paint to cover the bottom half. Have your child glue the triangle so that it creates the whale's tail! Finally have them glue on two googly eyes to the side of the plate that is painted black!	Sensory Bag: Fill a Ziploc bag with some shaving cream. Add a few drops of washable blue and yellow paint! Make sure it is sealed and then tape it to the table. Have your child use their fingers to mix the colors together to create a new color!	Kick Ball Play a game of kickball with your child! Simply roll the ball to them and have them kick it as hard as they can! See if they can round the bases before you tag them out! Make sure to take turns!	Trace 24 Using broken lines ---write down the number 24 on a regular sheet of print/lined paper (at least 10 times). Have your child use a washable marker to trace the number 24.	W is for Whale Craft! -paper plate -black construction paper -black and white washable paint -paint brush -googly eyes -scissors Sensory Bag: -Ziploc Bag -washable blue and yellow paint -shaving Cream Kick Ball -Child sized soccer ball -Lay out some bean bags to serve as bases (4) Try to include other family members for this game! Trace 24 -black pen/marker

						-regular sheet of paper -washable marker/cray on
Tuesday	The letter of the week: Ww

Number of the Week:24

Color of the Week: Green (Color Mixing)

Shape of the Week: Cube

Your Choice Book! | Build a Cube!

Using a green construction paper cut out 6 squares! They should all be the same size.

Help your child to glue them together to form a cube! | Sensory Bottle :

Fill a water bottle or store bought sensory bottle with water, a couple of drops of green food coloring , two drops of baby oil and some sparkles.

Make sure that the lid is tightly closed shut before giving it to your child! | Dodge Ball!

Play a game of dodgeball using some green balloons! | Cheerios and Pipe Cleaners!

Give your child a bowl of dry cheerios and 3 pipe cleaners to lace.

When they are done lacing, help them to bend their pipe cleaners so that they look like the letter W! | Build a cube! -green construction paper -glue -scissors

Sensory Bottle: -water bottle or store bought sensory bottle -water -green food coloring -sparkles -baby oil

Dodgeball -green balloons!

Build some worms! -bowl of dry cheerios -3 pipe cleaners! |

Wednesday	The letter of the week: Ww Number of the Week:24 Color of the Week: Green (Color Mixing) Shape of the Week: Cube Your Choice Book	Decorate your cube! Give your child a cube shaped box. Have them decorate their cube with some valentine's day themed stickers!	Sensory Bin: Fill your bin with the following: -kinetic sand -heart shaped cookie cutters (kid friendly).	Silly Hat Dance Party! Play your child's favorite dance music! Have a dance party while wearing some silly hats!	Valentine's Day Buddy! Give your child a water bottle. Have them use a tweezer to fill it up with some red pomp poms! Once the bottle is full, put the lid back on tightly. Have your child add two googly and a happy smile with a red washable marker!	Decorate your Cube! -cube shaped box -valentine's day themed stickers! Sensory Bin: -plastic bin large enough to fit 3 pairs of shoes -kinetic sand -child friendly heart shape cookie cutters Silly Hat Dance! -child's favorite dance music -silly hats! Valentine's Day Buddy! -empty water bottle - red fuzzy pom poms -googly eyes -red washable marker -child friendly tweezers
Thursday	The letter of the week: Ww Number of the Week :24 Color of the Week: Green (Color Mixing)	Chocolate Kiss Craft! Draw a large triangle on a piece of pink construction paper. It should be at least half of the size of the page. Precut some small pieces of	Sensory Bin: Fill your bin up with the following: -pink or red gift box filler -red heart paper doilies	Play a game of tag with your child! Make sure to take turns being the chaser!	Using a black marker/ pen draw 5 broken lines -----across a regular sheet of print/lined paper. These will serve as a guide for your child. Give them a pair of child friendly	Chocolate Kiss Craft -pink construction paper -black marker to draw the triangle -precut strips of aluminum foil -glue Valentine's Day Bin Pink/Red gift box filler paper -Red/White paper heart shaped doilies Play a game of tag!

	Shape of the Week: Cube Your Choice Book!	aluminum foil! Have your child glue the pieces of aluminum foil so that it covers the inside of the triangle.			scissors and have them cut along your drawn lines.	Practice Cutting -regular sheet of paper -pen/marker -child friendly scissors
Friday	The letter of the week: Ww Number of the Week :24 Color of the Week: Green (Color Mixing) Shape of the Week: Cube Your Choice Book!	Sponge Painting: Mixing Colors Give your child a clean dry sponge. Have them dip the sponge in some washable blue paint! Have them stamp their sponge on a white construction piece of paper to create multiple blue rectangles Have them dip a second sponge into some yellow paint to create	Sensory Bin: Fill your bin with the following: -dry green peas -plastic funnels -plastic different sized bowls	Croquet You will need 6 buckets and 3 pool noodles Bend the pool noodles so that each end is placed in 2 different buckets. Cushion the bucket so that the noodle forms an upright hoop. -Give your child a play plastic	Flour Letters Place a plastic mat on your table. Add ½ cup of flour to the mat! Have your child spread the flour with their hands. Have them practice writing the letters of the alphabet.	Sponge Painting: Mixing Colors -washable blue, and yellow paint -2 dry sponges -white construction paper Sensory Bin: -plastic bin large enough to fit 3 pairs of shoes. -uncooked green peas -plastic funnels -different sized plastic bowls Always supervise your child when working with small objects that may pose choking hazard. Croquet -3 pool noodles -6 buckets

| | | multiple yellow rectangles.

Finally have them dip the same sponge into yellow and blue paint so that the colors mix! Have them stamp with their new color! | | mallet and a ball! Have them maneuver the ball through the hoops with the plastic mallet for a fun game of Croquet! | | -bucket cushion ex) bean bags, small pillows, etc.

Flour Letters
-plastic mat
-1/2 cup |

Weather Theme Week: 1

	Circle Time	Craft	Sensory	Gross Motor	Fine Motor	Materials Needed
Monday	The letter of the week: Xx Number of the Week :25 Color of the Week: Orange (Color Mixing) Shape of the Week: Prism Your Choice Book!	X is for X-ray Using a black piece of construction paper and a white piece of chalk trace your child's hand. Have them glue on Q-Tips one per finger and add four of them to the palm of their hand!	Place a plastic mat on your table. Add a blob of shaving cream. Have your child play with some fluffy shaving cream clouds!	Give your child some colorful tissue paper! Have them pretend that they are tornadoes! Have them turn around in circles around the room while holding the long pieces of color full tissue paper! Make sure to remove any clutter to avoid tripping! Only a few times so that they don't get too dizzy!	Cotton Ball Clouds Using a black marker and a blue piece of construction paper write down the letter X (10 times). Write the letter in different areas of the paper. Have your child tear apart some cotton balls, then have them glue them onto the letter X.	X is for X-ray -black construction paper -Q-tips -glue -white chalk Shaving Cream Clouds -plastic mat -shaving cream Turn like a Tornado! -2 long colorful sheets of tissue paper Cotton Ball Clouds -blue construction paper -cotton balls -marker to write down the letter X -glue
Tuesday	The letter of the week: Xx	Sunny Day Using a white piece of constructio	Sensory: Tiny Tornado! Fill an empty water bottle with some	Flashlight Fun! Using a black marker,	Tracing Lighting Bolts! Using a black	Sunny Day -white construction paper

	Number of the Week :25 Color of the Week: Orange (Color Mixing) Shape of the Week: Triangular Prism Your Choice Book!	n paper and a black marker draw a circle in the middle of the paper. It should be about the size of a large soup bowl (This will be the sun). Use broken lines --- to draw the rays around the sun Have your child use a yellow dotter to cover the inside of the circle. Have them use a small paint brush to trace the rays of the sun!	water a little more than half way. Add a drop of liquid soap and a drop of food coloring (your color choice). Close the bottle and make sure it is sealed tightly. Turn the bottle upside down and shake in a circular motion. A small tornado should appear in the bottle!	write down the number 25 on regular sheets of print/lined paper (5 sheets total). Tape the sheets up in a room where the blinds can be drawn. Make sure to place them in different locations ex) under a chair, on a pillow, under a desk etc. Close the blinds and give your child a flashlight! Make sure you have a flashlight of your own! Always more fun with two flashlights! Go hunting for number 25 with your flashlights!	marker and regular sheet of print/lined paper draw 4 large zig zag lines across the page (make sure to spread them out!) Give child a yellow crayon and have them trace the lightning bolts!	-yellow washable paint dotter -yellow washable paint -small paint brush -black marker Tiny Tornado! -empty water bottle -food coloring of choice -liquid soap Flashlight Fun -flashlights -5 regular sheets of paper -black marker -tape Make sure that the room has enough light to avoid tripping over any objects. It shouldn't be pitch black just a little dark. Tracing Lighting Bolts -regular sheet of print/lined paper -black marker -yellow crayon

| Wednesday | The letter of the week: Xx

Number of the Week :25

Color of the Week: Orange (Color Mixing)

Shape of the Week: Triangular Prism

Your Choice Book! | Cloudy Day

Using a black marker draw a circle in the middle of a blue piece of construction paper.

The circle will be the sun!

Add a drop of red and yellow paint to the center.

Have your child use a paint brush to mix the two colors together. Have them paint the inside area of the circle with their new mixed color.

Once the paint has dried have them glue on some cotton balls to either side of the circle. Also add a few cotton balls | Hurricane in a Glass

Fill a clear plastic cup with water

Add a drop of blue food coloring and a drop of red food coloring

Watch the colors drop and mix on their own!

It's a hurricane of colors! | Number puddles!

Using blue construction paper (5 pieces), and a black marker write down numbers 21 through 25. One number per sheet.

Tape them down the floor!

Make sure to space them out so that your child has enough room to hop to each number. | Triangular Prisms

Using Magnetic Tile Blocks

Help your child to build triangular prisms | Cloudy Day
-blue construction paper
-black marker
-yellow and red washable paint
-paint brush
-glue
-cotton balls

Hurricane in a Glass
-plastic clear cup
-water
-blue and red food coloring

Number Puddles:
-black marker
-blue construction paper
-tape

Triangular Prisms:
-magnetic tile blocks |

		to the middle of the circle. It's a cloudy Day				
Thursday	The letter of the week: Xx Number of the Week: 25 Color of the Week: Orange (Color Mixing) Shape of the Week: Triangular Prism Your Choice Book!	Kite Craft Cut a diamond shape out of a white piece of construction paper! Cut 3 long strips of orange tissue paper. Have your child dip their fingers into some washable finger paint of their choice! Have them decorate the body of their kite with their fingerprints! When the paint is dry have them glue on the strips of tissue paper to the bottom of the kite	Thunderstorm! Give your child a reusable baking aluminum pan a plastic soup spoon, and a flash light! Have them hit the aluminum pan with their spoon to make thunder sounds and then flashlight to create lighting!	Fly your Kite! Have your child run through the yard as fast as they can while holding onto the kite string!	Trace the Letter X Using a black marker and a regular sheet of print/ lined paper draw the letter X (10 times)using broken lines ----- Have your child use a washable marker (their choice color) to trace the letter "X"	Kite Craft: -white construction paper -finger-paints -yarn -hole puncher -orange tissue paper Thunderstorm! -reusable aluminum pan -plastic large soup soon -flashlight Fly Your Kite -This week's kite craft! Trace the letter "X" -black marker -regular sheet of print/lined paper -washable marker

		(these are the kite tails) Use a hole puncher to punch a hole through the other end of the kite and tie a string of yarn long enough so your child can fly their kite!				
Friday	The letter of the week: Xx Number of the Week :25 Color of the Week: Orange (Color Mixing) Shape of the Week :Triangular Prism Your Choice Book!	Paint A Rainbow! Using a black marker and a white piece of construction paper draw 4 semi circles one inside of the other. The largest semi-circle should take up at least half of the page. Have your child use washable paint to create a beautiful rainbow!	Sensory Bin: Beans and Lighting bolts Fill your bin with the following: -black beans, -different sized plastic cups -twisted pieces of aluminum foil	5X5=25 Put some upbeat music on and have a workout session with your child! Cheer each other on! 5 Jumping Jacks 5 Hops 5 lunges 5 high knees 5 toe touches Safety first! Make sure your child is comfortable doing the movements and that	Name Trace Using a black marker and white construction paper write your child's first name. Make the letters large enough so that your child can trace them with a dotter.	Paint a Rainbow -washable paints 4 colors of choice -black marker -white construction paper -paint brush Sensory Bin: -plastic bin large enough to fit 3 pairs of shoes -aluminum foil -black beans -different sized plastic cups Always supervise your child when working with small objects 5x5=25

					they stay hydrated!		-up beat music Invite the rest of the family to join in! 5 Jumping Jacks 5 Hops 5 lunges 5 high knees 5 toe touches Name Trace: -white construction paper -dotter (child's choice of color) -black marker

Weather Theme Week: 2

	Circle Time	Craft	Sensory	Gross Motor	Fine Motor	Materials Needed
Monday	The letter of the week: Yy Number of the Week: 26 Color of the Week: Grey (Color Mixing) Emotion of the Week: Happy Shape Review: Circle Your Choice Book!	Y is for Yellow! Using a black marker draw a large circle on a white piece of paper. It should take up at least half of the paper. Have your child use a yellow dotter to fill the circle. When the paint is dry have them glue two googly eyes. Have them use a black washable marker to draw on a happy smile!	Rain in a Cup Fill a plastic clear cup half way with water. Fill the rest of the cup with some shaving cream. Add some drops of blue paint on top of the shaving cream! Watch it rain in your cup!	Rainbow Hop Place green, blue, red, pink, and yellow construction paper on the floor! Make sure to tape them down! Make sure to space them out far enough so your child can hop from color to color!	Letter Review Using a black marker write down letters A –Y on white construction paper Have your child dip their finger in some washable paint (kids color choice) Have them identify each letter as they finger paint!	Y is for yellow! -black washable marker -googly eyes -yellow dotter - Rain in a Cup -Clear plastic cup -shaving cream -blue washable paint -water Rainbow Hop -green, yellow, blue, pink, red construction paper squares -tape Letter Review - washable finger paint! -white construct

					ion paper. -black marker
Tuesday	The letter of the week: Yy

Number of the Week: 26

Color of the Week: Grey (Color Mixing)

Emotion of the Week: Happy

Shape review :Circle

Your Choice Book! | Tornado patterns

Using a black marker and a white construction paper draw 4 rectangles

Make it so that the largest rectangle is on top. Scale them down as you get to the bottom so that it looks like a funnel.

Have your child color each box using a paint brush and some black and white washable paint.

Have them create an alternating black and white color pattern tornado. | Fill a Ziploc bag with some shaving cream. Add some drops of white and black washable paint.

Make sure that the bag is sealed and tape it to the table.

Have your child mix the colors together with their fingers to create a new color! | Happy Face Wall Balls!

Using a black marker and a yellow piece of paper draw a large happy face and tape it on the wall.

Give your child a bouncy ball!

Have them list things that make them happy as they bounce the ball of the wall! | Shapes and Pom- Poms!

Using a black marker and a regular sheet of print/lined paper draw the following shapes :

-pentagon -oval -rectangle -triangle -hexagon

Give your child some fuzzy pom poms.

Have them identify each shape and glue a pom pom on each | Tornado Pattern: -white construct ion paper -black marker -black and white washable paint -paint brush

Sensory Bag: -white and black white washable paint -Ziploc bag -tape -shaving cream

Happy Face Wall Balls -yellow paper -black marker -bouncy ball -tape

Shapes and Pom- Poms |

					-fuzzy pom-poms -regular sheet of paper -black marker
Wednesday	The letter of the week: Yy Number of the Week: 26 Color of the Week: Grey (Color Mixing) Emotion of the Week: Happy Shape Review: Circle Your Choice Book!	Wind Chime! Give your child an empty toilet paper roll. Have them decorate their roll with some glue and fuzzy pom poms. Give them some precut strips of colorful tissue paper. Have them glue the strips to one of the ends of their roll. Use a hole puncher to poke a hole through the other end of the roll and tie a string of yarn to it!	Snow in a bottle Fill a plastic bottle half way with some water. Add a few drops of baby oil. Add some silver glitter and some white washable paint drops. Seal the bottle tightly before giving it to your child.	Using side walk chalk draw 4 large squares. On the first square draw the letter Y On the second draw 26 On the third draw a happy face On the 4th draw a diamond. Give your child a bouncy ball! Have a game of four square with some family members! Make sure to call out the item on the square before the ball is tossed to the	Counting Clouds! Give your child a bowl of marshmallows. Set an empty plastic cup next to the bowl. Have them practice counting to 26 as they transfer the marshmallows with their fingers.	Wind Chime -empty roll of toilet paper -fuzzy pom poms -glue -tissue paper strips -string of yarn -hole puncher Snow in a Bottle: -plastic clear bottle -water -baby oil -silver glitter -drops of white washable paint 4 Square Review! -sidewalk chalk -bouncy ball

				person on the square! Counting Clouds -plastic bowl -marshma llows -plastic cup		4 family members
Thursday	The letter of the week: Yy Number of the Week:26 Color of the Week: Grey (Color Mixing) Emotion of the Week: Happy Shape Review: Circle Your choice Book!	Grey Rain Cloud Using a black marker and white construction paper draw horizontal large oval towards the top of the paper. Place a few drops of black and white washable paint in the center. Have your child mix the colors with a paint brush and then cover the inside area of the oval with their mixed color. When they are done	Sensory Bin Fill your bin with the following: -water -grey Stones -Plastic funnels -different sized plastic cups	Musical Chairs! Play a game of musical chairs with your child! Play their favorite dance music as your circle the chairs!	Face Trace Using a black marker and a white piece of paper draw a happy face and sad face using broken lines -------. Give them a mirror and have them make a happy and a sad face. Ask them to describe a time when they felt sad. Ask t them to describe a time when they felt happy. Have them trace the faces using a	Grey Cloud -black and white washable paint -white construct ion paper -marker -washable blue finger-paint Sensory Bin: -plastic bin large enough to fit 3 pairs of shoes -grey stones/p ebbles -water -plastic funnels -different sized plastic cups

		have them dip their finger in some blue finger paint and create rain drops below the cloud!			washable marker. Always supervise your child when playing with small items that can pose choking hazard! Musical Chairs -Child Sized chair -favorite music Face Trace -white paper -black marker -hand held mirror Always supervise your child when using breakable items.	
Friday	The letter of the week: Yy Number of the Week :26 Color of the Week: Grey	Fan Fun! Using a paper plate and a black marker write the letter "26" in multiple	Sensory Play: Fill your bin with the following:	Over and Under Obstacle Course! Create an obstacle course using	Happy Picture Ask your child to name an activity makes them happy.	Fan Fun -different color washable paint dotters -black marker

	(Color Mixing) Emotion of the Week: Happy Shape Review: Circle Your Choice Book!	areas of the paper. Give your child different color dotters. Have them dot the number 26. Once they dot all of the numbers have them add some more dots so that the page looks extra colorful. Tape the paper plate to the top of popsicle stick!	-plastic funnels Rainbow rice: (Fill 3 Ziploc bags with rice. In each bag add a few drops of washable paint (each bag should be a different color). Mix the bags with the paint. Use a plastic mat to spread and dry the contents. Once it is dry pour the colored rice into the bin.	large pillows and chairs. Have your child climb over the pillows and under the chairs!	Give them some crayons and a regular sheet of print paper. Have you child draw a picture of their happy activity. Ex) baking cookies with grandma, playing soccer, reading books, etc.	-paper plate -popsicle stick -glue Sensory Bin: plastic bin large enough to fit 3 pairs of shoes - rainbow rice -plastic funnels Over and Under Obstacle Course -Large Pillows -Chairs Happy Picture -regular sheet of print paper and crayons

Weather Theme Week: 3

	Circle Time	Craft	Sensory	Gross Motor	Fine Motor	Materials Needed
Monday	The letter of the week: Zz Number of the Week: 27 Color of the Week: purple (Color Mixing) Emotion of the Week: Mad Shape Review: Rectangle Your Choice Book	Z is for Zebra Using a black marker and a yellow construction paper draw a large letter Z. It should take up at least half of the paper. Have your child dot letter Z using a white and black washable paint dotter. Make sure they alternate the colors to form a pattern. Have them glue on two googly eyes. Have them add some black strands of yarn to the back of letter Z for some fun the zebra hair!	Fill a Ziploc bag with some shaving cream! Add a few drops of washable red and blue paint. Make sure the bag is sealed, then tape it to the table. Have your child mix the colors to create a new color!	Purple Paint Dance Party! Roll out a large piece of butcher paper. Paint the bottom of your child's feet with some washable purple paint. Put on some fun dance music and have a dance paint party!	Using a paper plate have your child create a grouchy face! Give your child some googly eyes, yarns for frowning eye brows. and Give them a washable marker to draw on the grouchy mouth. As they are working as them to tell you about a time when they felt mad or grouchy.	Zebra Craft -yellow Construction paper -black marker -washable black and white dotters -googly eyes -black strands of yarn Sensory Bag -Shaving Cream -blue and red washable paint -Ziploc bag -tape Purple Paint Dance Party -washable purple paint -large piece of butcher paper Grouchy Face -paper plate -yarn strands (child color choice) -googly eyes -washable marker

| Tuesday | The letter of the week: Zz

Number of the Week :27

Color of the Week: purple (Color Mixing)

Emotion of the Week: Mad

Shape Review: Rectangle

Your Choice Book! | Grapes!

Have your child dip one of the ends of an empty roll of toilet paper in some washable purple paint.

Have them stamp their roll onto a piece of yellow construction paper.

Help them to group their stamps together to make it look like a bunch of purple grapes! | Painting Crushed Ice!

Fill your sensory bin with the following:

-crushed ice

-paint brushes

-washable purple, red, blue, and yellow paint | Follow the Leader!

Play an active game of follow the leader with your child!

Example: dance, hop, skip, wave your hands!

Take turns being the leader! | Number Hail Storm!

Use a black marker to write numbers 20-27 on a piece of blue construction paper.

Have your child dip a Q-tip into some white paint.

Have them identify and dot each number. | Purple Grapes
-empty toilet paper roll
-washable purple paint
-yellow construction paper

Painting Crushed Ice
Sensory bin:
-plastic bin large enough to fit 3 pairs of shoes

-crushed ice
-washable paint: purple, blue, red, and yellow

Number Hail Storm!
-black marker
-blue construction paper
-white washable paint
-Q-tips

Follow the Leader Game
Make sure to be extra lively! |
|---|---|---|---|---|---|---|
| Wednesday | The letter of the week: Zz

Number of the Week: 27 | Sphere Art

Add drops of purple, red, and blue washable paint to the center of a | Sensory Bin

Fill your bin with the following:

-water | When we are mad exercise!

Have your child repeat and perform the | Lego Patterns

Have your child create color patterns with red | Sphere Art
-white construction paper
-hand sized ball
-washable blue, red, and purple paint |

	Color of the Week: purple (Color Mixing) Emotion of the Week: Mad Shape Review: Rectangle Your Choice Book!	white piece of construction paper. Give your child a hand sized ball. Have them create a beautiful painting by rolling their ball around the paper.	-shaving cream -bath toy boats Give your child some Plastic straws. Have your child blow into the straw to create some wind for their boats!	following exercise! When we are angry we Feel like we want to stomp like an elephant! (Stomp, Stomp, Stomp) When we are mad sometimes we want to roar like a Lion (Let out a big roar). When we are mad sometimes we want to wave our hands like we are swatting bees! (swat, Swat, swat) -But then we take a big breath and blow out a pretend balloon (inhale, exhale,	and blue Lego blocks.	Sensory Bin: -plastic bin big enough to fit 3 pairs of shoes -bath toy boats -shaving cream -water -straws When We are Mad Exercise -just yourselves! Lego Block Color Patterns Legos: Red and Blue

				slowly three times) And it makes us feel better.		
Thursday	The letter of the week: Zz Number of the Week: 27 Color of the Week: purple (Color Mixing) Emotion of the Week: Mad Shape review :Rectangle Your Choice Book!	Color Patterns Give your child some precut blue, red, and purple tissue paper squares. On a white piece of construction paper use a black marker to draw a large number 27. It should take up the full page. Have your child decorate the number 27 with a red, blue, and purple pattern.	Sensory Bin: Fill your bin with the following: -dry rainbow colored cereal -plastic funnels -plastic measuring cups	Bobsled Race! You will need 2 laundry baskets. One for you and one for your child. Fill them with stuffed animals! Push your baskets across the room and back as fast as you can! First one to the finish line wins!	Shape Patterns Have your child create some fun shape patterns using geometric tiles!	Color Patterns -white construction paper -black marker -blue, red, purple, tissue paper squares -glue Sensory Bin: -plastic bin large enough to fit 3 pairs of shoes -plastic funnels -plastic measuring cups -rainbow dry cereal Bobsled race -2 laundry baskets -stuffed animals Shape Patterns! If you do not have geo blocks simply cut out some shapes using construction paper. Your choice of 2 shapes. Ex) Oval, square, Oval Square...etc.

| Friday | The letter of the week: Zz

Number of the Week :27

Color of the Week: purple (Color Mixing)

Emotion of the Week: Mad

Shape Review Rectangle

Your Choice Book! | Toast with Grape Jam!

Using a black marker draw a large rectangle on a white piece of construction paper. The shape should take up the full page.

Have your child use a paint brush to trace the lines of the paper with brown washable paint.

Next have them dip their brush in some purple washable paint to fill in the inside of the shape! | Sensory Bin:

Fill your bin with the following:

-water

-ping pong balls

-purple food coloring

-plastic bowls

-plastic spoons | Jump Over

Using a black marker Write down numbers 1-10 on plastic cups (1 number per cup).

Place them on the floor. Space them out so that there is enough room for your child to jump over each cup!

Have your child jump over each cup while counting. | Purple Flower Petals

Have your child tear some purple tissue paper.

Using a black marker draw a circle on a piece of white construction paper. It should be the size of your hand. Have them color the inside of the circle with a yellow crayon.

Have them trace the circle with their torn tissue paper. | Toast with Grape Jam!
-white construction paper
-purple and brown washable paint
-paint brush
-black marker

Sensory Bin
-plastic sensory bin large enough to fit 3 pairs of shoes

-ping pong balls

-purple food coloring

-plastic large spoons and bowls

Jump Over
-black marker
-plastic cups

Purple Flower Petals
-purple tissue paper
-black marker
-white construction paper |

Weather Theme Week: 4

	Circle Time	Craft	Sensory	Gross Motor	Fine Motor	Materials Needed
Monday	Sight Word "AT"

Number of the Week :28

Color of the week: Yellow and Green Review

Emotion of the Week: Sad

Shape :Triangle Review

Your Choice Book! | ABC Storm!

Using a black piece of construction paper and white chalk draw letters A - Z throughout the paper.

Have your child dip their finger in some blue washable paint. Have them identify and dot each letter.

Give them some crinkle strips of aluminum foil

Have them glue the foil onto the paper.

Next have them glue on some cotton balls for clouds! | Fill a bowl with some baking soda.

Fill a separate paper cup with some white vinegar and yellow food coloring

Fill a separate cup with white vinegar and some Green food coloring.

Have your child use child friendly pipettes to carefully drop the colorful mixture of vinegar into the bowl of baking soda for some fizzy fun! | Aim at "AT"

On a regular sheet of paper write down the word "At". Make it large enough for your child to see from across the room.

Tape it to the wall.

Give your child a bucket of bouncy walls!

Have them take aim at "AT". | Dotting "At"

Using a black marker and a regular sheet of paper write down the word "at" multiple times in different areas of the paper.

Have your child use a dotter to dot the word "at".

Have them read the word out loud each time they stamp it! | ABC Storm - aluminu m foil -black construct ion paper -white chalk -blue washable finger- paint -cotton balls

Fizzy Fun! 2 child Friendly pipettes -baking soda -green and yellow food coloring -white vinegar

Aim at "AT" -regular paper -tape -bucket -bouncy balls |

					-marker/pen Dotting At: -regular sheet of paper -dotter (child's choice of color) -black marker
Tuesday	Sight Word "AT" Number of the Week: 28 Color of the week: Yellow and Green Review Emotion of the Week: Sad Shape: Triangle Review Your Choice Book!	28 Triangles! Using green construction paper cut mini triangles (28). Tip: Fold the paper so that you that you can cut out the triangles in one or two rounds of cuts! It's a time saver! On a blue piece of construction paper draw a large triangle (Should pretty much take up the whole paper). Have your child glue their mini triangles inside the large triangle to fill the inside area! Once they are glued have	Number Squish Bag Fill a Ziploc bag with some clear hair gel and some plastic play numbers! At least five different numbers Make sure the bag is sealed and tape it onto the table. Have your child identify each number and move them around to combine them to form different numbers.	Obstacle Course Create an Over Under obstacle course using chairs, yarn and pillows. Tie a piece of yarn to two chairs (make sure there is enough room for your child to go under the yarn. Place a pillow on the floor and have them hop over. Replicate this setting a total of 3 times.	Sad Face Using a black marker and a piece of white construction paper draw a circle the size of a large bowl. Give your child some washable black paint and a small brush. Help them to draw a sad face. Dip their finger in some	28 Triangles -blue and green construction paper -scissors -glue Number Squish Bag -Ziploc bag -plastic play numbers -tape -clear hair gel Over Under Obstacle Course -6 Chairs -Yarn -3 pillows Sad Face -white piece of

					washable blue finger-paint to dot some tears on the face. As they are working talk about a time when they felt sad.	construction paper -black marker - washable blue paint - washable black paint
Wednesday	Sight Word "AT" Number of the Week :28 Color of the week: Yellow and Green Review Emotion of the Week: Sad Shape: Triangle Review Your Choice Book!	Shape Patterns Using green and yellow construction paper cut a total of 10 triangles. 5 green triangles and 5 yellow triangles Have your child create an alternating pattern of green and yellow. Have them glue the pattern onto a piece of black construction paper.	Sensory Bottle: Fill an empty plastic bottle a little more than half way with some water. Add a couple of drops of baby oil. Add a drop of yellow food coloring and a little bit of green litter. Make sure the bottle is completely and securely sealed before giving it to you child.	Fun with Rainbow Handkerchiefs! Give your child some colorful handkerchiefs to hold! Have them move their arms like windmills! Have them turn like tornadoes! Have them run as fast as they can while holding their hankies up so that they catch the air!	Connect the Words! Fold a regular sheet of paper in half vertically. Using a black marker/pen write the word "at" on either side of the paper write the word at at at at at	Shape Patterns -yellow, green, and black construction paper -glue -scissors Sensory Bottle: -green glitter -yellow food coloring -water -baby oil -plastic bottle - Fun with Rainbow Handkerchiefs -colorful handkerchiefs

					at at Give your child a washable marker to draw a horizontal or diagonal line to connect the words on the opposite side	Connect the Words -regular sheet of paper -black marker/pen -washable marker
Thursday	Sight Word "AT" Number of the Week:28 Color of the week: Yellow and Green Review Emotion of the Week: Sad Shape: Triangle Review Your Choice Book!	Overcast Sky Using a blue construction paper add a few drops of white and grey washable paint in the center. Give your child a play dough roller. Have them use the roller to spread the paint across the paper to create an over cast sky!	Sensory Bin: Fill your bin with the following: -shaving cream -plastic toy airplanes	ABC Body Stretch From a standing position have your child form a letter T with their arms Have them sit and form the letter L Have them lie down on the mat and form the letter V in a toe touch! Make sure to have your own mat and do the fun	Board Books! Set up a quiet reading area. Use some pillows, bean bags, or set up a comfy chair! Play some classical music in the background Give your child some fun	Overcast Sky! -blue construction paper -white and grey washable paint -play roller Sensory Bin: Plastic bin large enough to fit 3 pairs of shoes -plastic toy planes -shaving cream

				stretches with them! Safety First! Make sure that your child is comfortable doing the exercises.	board books! Have them flip through the pages of their book!	ABC Stretch -floor yoga mats Always take your child's ability into account. Remember safety first! Board Books! - pillows/beanbags/comfy chair -classical music -Have your child choose their favorite board books to flip through.
Friday	Sight Word "AT" Number of the Week :28 Color of the week:	Gloomy Face Craft! Have your child paint a paper cup with yellow washable paint.	Sensory Bin Add the following to your sensory bin: -water -green food -bath bubbles	Over, Under, Around. Set up an obstacle course! Use items of your choice, but make sure to make it so that the	Colorful Rock Patterns! Give your child some rocks and some green and	Gloomy Face Craft! -paper cup -googly eyes -glue -blue washable paint

	Yellow and Green Review Emotion of the Week: Sad Shape: Triangle Review Your Choice Book!	Flip the cup upside down. Have them add some googly eyes to the side of the cup. Have them use a washable black marker to draw on a sad smile. Have them dip their finger in some blue washable paint to dot some tears on their gloomy monster. Have them glue on some strands of blue yarn to the cup for hair!	-yellow and green Legos	directions of over, under, and around are followed. Also, make extra sure that all materials used are child friendly. Safety First! EX) Jump over the cup, run around the chair, and crawl under the table!	yellow washable paint. Have them use a small brush to cover the rocks with paint. Once they have dried have them create an alternating color pattern.	-yellow washable paint -blue yarn -paint brush Sensory Bin: -water -green food coloring -yellow and green Legos -bath bubbles Over, Under, and Around Recommended items: table, chair, paper cup. Colorful Rock Patterns -green and yellow washable paint -paint brush -rocks (10)

						Always supervise your child when working with small objects that may pose choking hazard.

Farm Animals Theme   Week: 1

	Circle Time	Craft	Sensory	Gross Motor	Fine Motor	Materials needed
Monday	Sight Word "HAT" Number of the Week :29 Color of the week: Pink and White Review Emotion of the Week: Mad Shape: Oval Review Your Choice Book!	Easter Oval Hard Boil an Egg and let it cool. Give your child the hardened egg. Give them some washable paint and a small brush. Have them paint their oval with the colors of their choice	Sensory Bin: Fill your sensory bin with the following: - dried oatmeal - plastic toy farm animals	Chasing Chickens! Fill up some white balloons. Using a black marker draw two eyes. Using an orange marker draw on a beak! Toss the balloons around the room. Have your child chase the chickens! Make sure to keep running around yourself tossing the balloons in the air as the chickens try to get away!	Using a black marker/ pen and a small notepad write down the word "at" and the word "hat" Place the notes inside plastic Easter eggs and close them up. Fill up about 6 eggs! Have your child open the eggs and sound out the words!	Easter Oval -Hardboiled egg -washable paint -small brush Sensory Bin -plastic bin large enough to fit 3 pairs of shoes -dry Oatmeal -plastic farm animal toys Chasing Chickens -white balloons -black and orange marker -Word Filling -marker/pen -notepad -plastic Easter eggs 6
Tuesday	Sight Word "HAT"	Fluffy Sheep! In the middle of a blue piece of	Muddy Pig! On a piece of pink construction paper draw	Word Jump! Using sidewalk chalk write down the	Counting with Carrots! Fill a bowl with some	Fluffy Sheep -blue and black construction paper -cotton balls

Number of the Week:29 Color of the week: Pink and White Review Emotion of the Week: Mad Shape: Oval Review Your Choice Book!	construction paper draw a bowl sized circle. Give your child 4 precut black construction paper rectangles (sheep legs) And 1 triangle (this will be the sheep's head) Give your child a bowl full of white cotton balls. Have your child glue on the triangle to the middle of the circle. Have them glue on the cotton balls around the triangle until the rest of the circle is filled. Have them glue on the rectangle legs to the bottom of the circle.	a circle the size of your hand (That's the head of the pig.) In the middle of that circle draw a smaller circle (that's the nose). Add two triangles to either side for ears. Have your child glue on some googly eyes. Using a black marker draw on a smile. Place your pig inside a large Ziploc bag. Add a few drops of brown washable paint. Seal the bag and tape it to the table. Have your child use their hands to move the	following words on the ground using sidewalk chalk: Hat At Cat Have your child identify and hop to each word!	baby carrots! Write the number 29 down on a piece of print/lined paper. It should take up the full page. Have your child use the carrots to trace 29. Make sure to have them count the contents of their bowl!	-glue Muddy Pig -pink construction paper -brown washable paint -googly eyes -black marker -Ziploc bag Word Jump -side walk chalk If you are doing this activity indoors write down words on a regular sheet of paper and tape them down securely to the floor. Counting with Carrots! -Plastic Bowl -Baby Carrots (29 if possible) -regular piece of paper -black marker/pen

			paint around so that it covers the pink pig!			
Wednesday	Sight Word "HAT" Number of the Week :29 Color of the week: Pink and White Review Emotion of the Week: Mad Shape: Oval Review Your Choice Book!	Baby Chick Craft Give your child a paper plate. Give your child some washable yellow paint. Have them use their paint brush to cover inside area of the plate yellow. Have them glue on 2 googly eyes Give them a precut orange construction paper triangle to glue on for the beak. Have them glue on a few yellow feathers to the rim of the plate.	Sheep Shearing! -On a black piece of construction paper use white chalk to draw an oval. Glue on two googly eyes and a smile. Cover the area around the oval with shaving cream. Give your child a plastic small comb. Have them sheer their sheep!	Easter Egg Color Sort Hide some colorful plastic Easter eggs around the house. Have your child collect all the eggs and then sort them out by color!	Build a Farm Using Legos and farm animal toys build a farm with animal pens.	Baby Chick Craft -paper plate -yellow washable paint -paint brush -yellow feathers -orange construction paper Sheep Sheering -black construction paper -googly eyes -white chalk -shaving cream -small plastic comb Build a Farm -Legos -plastic farm animal toys Easter Egg Color Sort -plastic Easter egg -basket
Thursday	Sight Word "HAT"	Give your child a paper plate	Bubbly Duck Pond	Lasso the Calf!	Write down the word "hat" multiple	Angry Hen! -black and orange

	Number of the Week :29 Color of the week: Pink and White Review Emotion of the Week: Mad Shape: Oval Review Your Choice Book!	Precut black rectangles for angry eyebrows Also precut a triangle from an orange construction paper to use as a beak. Have your child dip a sponge into some red washable paint. Have them cover the inside area of the plate red. Have them glue on two googly eyes And the triangle beak. Help them glue on the eye brows so that they are diagonal creating a frown \/ As they are creating their craft talk about a time when something	Fill your sensory bin with some water Add a few rubber duckies Add some bath bubbles	Form a lasso out of jump rope! Set up a small chair! Have your child lasso the calf before he gets away!	times on a piece of paper. Give your child some Easter themed stickers and have them place a sticker on each word. Make sure they read the word before placing the sticker.	construction paper -red washable paint -dry sponge -glue -googly eyes Duck Pond -Sensory Bin -plastic bin large enough to fit 3 pairs of shoes -water -bath bubbles -rubber ducks Lasso the Calf -Jump Rope -Small Chair Always supervise your child to make sure they are playing safe! Easter Stickers and Hat! -regular sheet of paper -Easter themed stickers - pen/marker

	made your child mad. Questions: What happened? How did it make you feel? What did you do?				to write down words
Friday	Sight Word "HAT" Number of the Week 29 Color of the week: Pink and White Review Emotion of the Week: Mad Shape: Oval Review Your Choice Book!	Pink and White Bunny You will need to precut two long ovals to be used for bunny ears Also, precut pink triangle for a nose using construction paper. Give your child a paper cup. Give your child some precut pink and white tissue paper squares. Have them glue the squares on the cup creating an alternating pattern of white and pink until	Sensory Bin Fill your bin with the following: -gardening soil -baby carrots -mini potatoes -toy rake and shovel	Easter Egg Spoon full of color! Set up 3 different colored construction papers on the floor. Tape them down. Give your child a container filed with plastic Easter eggs matching the colors of the paper you have chosen. There should be at least 2 eggs of each color. Give your child a plastic spoon.	Salt Tray Writing Fill a paper or plastic tray with some salt Have your child practice writing the word hat with their finger	Pink and White Bunny -paper cup -white and pink tissue paper squares -pink construction paper -white construction paper -glue -googly eyes -1 cotton ball Sensory Bin: -plastic bin large enough to fit 3 pairs of shoes -gardening soil -baby carrots -mini potatoes -toy mini rake -toy mini shovel

| | | the cup is covered.

Have them add two googly eyes

Have them glue the triangle nose, then have them add the two ovals for ears.

Finally add a cotton ball for the tail. | | Have them place one egg on the spoon and power walk over to the paper with the matching color. They are to place their egg on the paper and repeat until all the eggs are on their matching colored paper! | | Easter Egg Spoon full of color!
-3 different colored pieces of construction paper
-plastic spoon
-plastic colorful Easter eggs that match the chosen colors of the construction paper (6-10)
-tape

Salt Tray Writing
-small plastic tray or paper plate
-salt |

Farm Animal Theme Week: 2

	Circle Time	Craft	Sensory	Gross Motor	Fine Motor	Materials Needed
Monday	Sight Word "CAT" Number of the Week:30 Color of the week: Blue and Orange Review Emotion of the Week: Surprised Shape: Square Review Your Choice Book!	Surprised Cat! Using construction paper Precut 2 black triangles (cat ears) An orange triangle (cat nose) And two white round circles to be used to form surprised eyes! Give your child a paper plate Have them dip a plastic fork in some washable black paint. Next have them stamp their painted fork plate until the inside area is completely covered.	Give your child a chilled orange First have your child look, feel, and smell it. Finally peel the orange, and have them taste it! Questions to ask: What color is it? How does it feel? Is it sweet? Is it sour?	Help your Child build a fort with chairs, pillows, and blankets!	Fruit Faces! Using 4 oranges and a washable black marker, have your child draw a happy sad, and a surprised face. One face per orange.	Surprised Cat! -black, orange and white construction paper -blue washable marker -black washable paint -plastic form -glue Orange Fruit Activity -chilled orange Note: Make sure that your child is not allergic to the fruit before giving them the orange! Build a Fort! -pillows -chairs -blankets -Make sure to supervise your child when building and playing! Safety first!

		Have them glue on the two black triangles on the side of the plate to create cat ears! Have them glue on the two white circles for eyes and the triangle nose. Have your child use a washable blue marker to dot the eyes.				Fruit Faces -4 oranges -washable black marker
Tuesday	Sight Word "CAT Number of the Week: 30 Color of the week: Blue and Orange Review Emotion of the Week: Surprised Shape: Square Review	Blue Square Craft! Using a black marker and a white construction paper draw a large square. It should take up most of the paper. Have your child use a blue dotter to fill the inside area of the square.	Sensory Bin Fill your bin with the following: -orange colored dry pasta! Fill a large Ziploc bag with pasta and a few drops of orange washable paint. Seal and shake the bag until the	Parachute! Place a large light blanket on the floor, then place a small bouncy ball in the center of the blanket. Have your child hold one end of the blanket while you hold the other end.	Creating Words Write down the word "cat" on a piece of regular paper. On a second piece of paper write down "at" Have your child practice creating the word cat with some plastic play	Blue Square Craft! -black marker -white construction paper -blue tissue paper -glue -Sensory Bin: -plastic bin large enough to fit 3 pairs of shoes

224

	Your Choice Book!	Have them tear pieces of blue of tissue paper. Have them glue the torn pieces of paper so that they trace the lines of the square.	pasta is covered, then spread out the pasta to dry on a plastic mat.) -different sized plastic cups	Together lift your arms to the sky and bring down the blanket. Watch the ball fly to the sky!	ABC letters. They should use the word on the paper as their guide.	-orange colored dry pasta -different sized plastic cups -Parachute -light large blanket -bouncy ball (Try to get a couple of added family members to participate in the game). Creating Words -2 sheets of paper -ABC plastic play letters (If you don't have play letters write the letters needed down on sticky notes).
Wednesday	Sight Word "CAT Number of the Week :30 Color of the week: Blue and Orange	Horse Handprints! Cover the inside of your child's hand with some washable brown paint!	Sensory Bin: Fill your bin with the following: -water -plastic Easter Eggs -blue food coloring	Collect the Chicken Eggs! Using a washable marker and plastic Easter eggs. Write down the words "CAT" and	Counting Jelly Beans! Fill a bowl with 30 Jelly Beans Have your child transfer the jelly beans to an empty	Horse Handprints -yellow construction pa per -brown washable paint -black washable paint -thin brush

	Review	Have them stamp their hand on a yellow construction paper.	-plastic spoons	"AT" on them.	bowl using their fingers while counting to 30.	
	Emotion of the Week: Surprised			3 eggs should say "CAT" and 3 should say "AT"		Sensory Bin: -plastic bin large enough to fit 3 pairs of shoes -water -blue food coloring -plastic Easter eggs -plastic spoons
	Shape: Square Review	Have them do it 3 times.				
	Your Choice Book!	Turn the paper over so that their fingerprints are facing the bottom of the page.		Place eggs in bowl on the floor. Place a pillow on top of the eggs (pretend it's a chicken).		Collect the Chicken Eggs! -plastic Easter eggs (6) -washable marker -basket -pillow -plastic bowl
		Next give them some washable black paint and a thin paint brush.		Give your child a basket to go collect the word eggs.		
		Have them draw some horse hair and a tail.		Finally have them separate the eggs according to the word written on them.		Counting Jelly Beans -2 Plastic Bowls -Jelly Beans
		The thumb print is the head and neck of the horse and the other 4 fingers are the legs!				Always supervise your child when working with small items that may cause choking hazard!

| Thursday | Sight Word "CAT" Number of the Week :30 Color of the week: Blue and Orange Review Emotion of the Week: Surprised Shape: Square Review Your Choice Book! | Handprint Cows! Using white washable paint cover the inside of your child's hand. Have them stamp their hand 3 times on blue construction paper. Turn the paper over so that their fingerprints are facing the bottom of the page The thumbs are the head and neck of the cows and the other 4 fingers are the legs. Give your child a thin brush and some black and brown washable paint. Have them draw on some horns and some | Sensory Bin: Fill your bin with the following: -blue dry pasta Fill a large Ziploc bag with pasta and a few drops of blue washable paint. Seal and shake the bag until the pasta is covered, then spread out pasta to dry on a plastic mat.) -different sized plastic cups | Have a Bunny Hop Race with your child! See who can hop to and from across the room first! Ready Set HOP!! | Draw a Picture! Set up a mirror in front of your child. Have them make a surprised face! Give them some crayons and a regular print paper. Have them draw a picture of their surprised face. As they are working talk about a time when they were surprised. Make sure to share a fun story about a time when you yourself were surprised as a guide for them! | Handprint Cows! -white and black washable paint -thin paint brushes. Sensory Bin: -plastic bin large enough to fit 3 pairs of shoes -blue dry pasta -different sized plastic cups Always supervise your child when working with small item that may pose choking hazard! Bunny Hop Race Just yourselves! Draw A Picture -crayons -paper -mirror Always supervise your child |

227

		spots on each cow.				when working with anything breakable! Safety First!
Friday	Sight Word "CAT" Number of the Week: 30 Color of the week: Blue and Orange Review Emotion of the Week: Surprised Shape: Square Review Your Choice Book!	Horse Puppet! Give your child a brown paper lunch bag. Have your child glue on two googly eyes to the bottom of the bag. Have them dip their fingers into some black washable paint to create nostrils beneath the eyes. Have them glue on some black yarn to the top and back of the bag for horse hair!	Sensory Bin: Fill your bin with the following: -water geometric tiles -orange food coloring -plastic scoops	Scarecrow Dance Put some fun dance music on! Have some fun dancing like a scarecrow! Sway your arms like a scarecrow in the wind! Wiggle your legs around like they are made out of rags! Let the wind turn you around and around!	Favorite Farm Animal. Give your child some regular print paper, and some washable markers. Ask them to draw a picture of their favorite farm animal.	Horse Puppet -brown paper lunch bag -glue -googly eyes -black washable paint - black yarn Sensory Bin: -plastic bin large enough to fit 3 pairs of shoes - water -geometric tiles -orange food coloring -plastic scoops Scarecrow Dance! -fun dance music -call out the following dance moves as the music plays: Sway your arms like a scarecrow in the wind!

						Wiggle your legs around like they are made out of rags! Let the wind turn you around and around! Have fun! Draw A Picture of your Favorite Farm Animal! -washable markers -regular sheet of paper

Farm Animal Theme Week: 3

Monday	Sight Word "HAT" Number of the Week :31 Color of the week: Purple Emotion of the Week: Fear Shape Review: Pentagon Your Choice Book!	Purple Pentagon Have your child use purple washable paint to paint 5 popsicle sticks! Have them glue the sticks onto a piece of construction paper to create a pentagon!	Place some Bubble Wrap on the floor! Have your child pop the bubbles with their feet!	Family Bike or Scooter Ride! Go out for a family bike or scooter ride around the neighborhood!	Easter Egg Basket! Using a whole puncher, punch holes around the rim of a paper bowl. Give your child some purple yarn to lace the bowl. Tie the ends of the yarn to form a bow. Have your child dip their finger in some washable purple, pink, yellow, and blue paint. Have them dot the inside the bowl to create colorful Easter eggs!	Purple Pentagon -5 popsicle sticks -purples washable paint -paint brush -white construction paper -glue Bubble Wrap Pop! -Bubble Wrap Family Scooter/Bike Ride! - Bike/Scooter Easter Egg Basket! -paper bowl -washable paint: blue, purple, pink, yellow -hole puncher -purple yarn

| Tuesday | Sight Word "HAT"

Number of the Week :31

Color of the week: Purple

Emotion of the Week: Fear

Shape Review: Pentagon

Your Choice Book! | Duckling Craft

Using orange construction paper, precut 2 orange triangles for feet! They should be about the size of your middle and index finger together.

Give your child a large paper cup!

Flip it over so it's upside down!

Give them some washable yellow paint!

Have them cover the outside area of their cup in yellow.

Have them glue on some yellow feathers to the side of the cup. | Purple Sensory Bottle:

Fill a water bottle with water (a little more than half way).

Add some purple food coloring.

Add a few drops of baby oil.

Add some glitter.

Seal the bottle tightly before giving it to your child. | Play a game of Duck! Duck! Goose!

Gather some family members in a circle!

Make sure everyone gets a chance to be the goose! | Scared Shapes!

On a white piece of construction paper draw a pentagon a rectangle and oval.

Each shape should be about the size of your hand.

Give your child some washable blue, red, and orange washable paint.

Have them trace the line of each shape with a different color.

Have them glue on two googly eyes to each shape.

Using washable black paint and a thin brush, have your child draw on a Draw on a | Duckling Craft
-washable orange and yellow paint
-yellow feathers
-glue
-paintbrush
-orange construction paper
- plastic/paper cup

Purple Sensory Bottle
-empty water bottle
-water
-baby oil
-glitter
-purple food coloring

Duck Duck Goose!

-Gather 3-4 family members or friends.

Scared Shapes
-white construction paper
-washable blue, red, orange, and black paint,
-think paint brush
-googly eyes |
|---|---|---|---|---|---|

		Have them glue on two googly eyes. Have them glue on two orange triangles on the bottom of the cup for feet. Have them use washable orange paint and a thin paint brush to draw on the beak.			crooked scared smile (Zigzag) to each shape. As they are working, talk about a time when they themselves felt scared.	-glue
Wednesday	Sight Word "HAT" Number of the Week :31 Color of the week: Purple Emotion of the Week: Fear Shape Review: Pentagon Your Choice Book!	Water Pail Craft! Precut some blue tissue paper squares Using a hole puncher, poke two holes on opposite sides of a paper plate bowl. Have your child use washable grey paint and a paintbrush to cover the outside of the pail.	Sensory Bin Fill your bin with the following: -dry corn kernels -plastic scoops -plastic farm animal toys Always supervise your child when working with small items that may pose choking hazard!	Ball Push! Cut 3 holes in a moving box. Make them large enough for a hand sized ball to fit through it. Using washable paints, trace one hole in blue paint, one in green paint, and one in red paint. Give your child some colorful plastic ball pit balls. Have them push the balls into the matching colors!	Trace 31 On a piece of construction paper write down the number 31. It should take up most of the page. Give your child a bowl of sunflower seeds. Have your glue the sunflower seeds so that that it traces the lines of the number.	Water Pail Craft! -hole puncher -paper plate bowl -grey washable paint -blue tissue paper squares -glue -pipe cleaner Sensory Bin: -dry corn kernels -plastic scoops -plastic farm animals Ball Push -moving Box

| | | Have them glue on the blue tissue paper squares to the inside area.

Have them lace a pipe cleaner to connect the two holes together and form a handle. | | | Have them count out loud to 31. | -15 ball pit balls: 5:green 5:blue 5:red -washable blue, red, and green paint -paint brush

If you do not have washable paint use markers.

Trace 31 -sunflower seeds -plastic bowl -glue - construction paper: any color

Always supervise your child when working with small items that may pose choking hazard! |
|---|---|---|---|---|---|---|
| Thursday | Sight Word "HAT"

Number of the Week 31 | Shape Mouse Craft!

Using a blue construction paper cut out a triangle | Sensory Bin

Fill your bin with the following:

-sunflower seeds | Avoid the Cat!

Using painter's tape create a zig zag pattern across the room. | Geoboards Fun!

Give your child a geoboard and some rubber bands! | Shape Mouse Craft! -blue construction paper -black washable paint |

| | Color of the week: Purple

Emotion of the Week: Fear

Shape Review: Pentagon

Your Choice Book! | (mouse face)

Cut out two circles (ears)

Have your child assemble and glue the mouse head onto a piece of white construction paper.

The triangle should be upside down and the two ears should be glued onto corners of the triangle.

Have them glue on two googly eyes.

Have them dip their finger in some washable pink paint and dot bottom of the triangle (that's the nose).

Have them use a thin paint brush to draw on some whiskers. | -small plastic shovels and plastic bowls | Have your child race across the room in a zig zag pattern as fast as the can! They are to pretend that they are a mouse running from the house cat!

Repeat 4 times!

Always make sure that your child is comfortable completing the exercise, and that they are hydrated! | Have them create some fun shapes! | -pink washable paint
-thin brush
-googly eyes
-glue

Sensory Bin:
-plastic bin large enough to fit 3 pairs of shoes
-sunflower seeds
-small plastic shovels and plastic bowls

Always supervise your child when working with small objects that may pose choking hazard!

Avoid the Cat!
-painter's tape

Geoboards Fun!
-Geoboard
-rubber bands

-Always supervise your child when playing with things that they could |

						potentially ingest.
Friday	Sight Word "HAT" Number of the Week :31 Color of the week: Purple Emotion of the Week: Fear Shape Review: Pentagon Your Choice Book!	Purple Flower Handprints! Cover the inside of your child's hand in purple washable paint. Have them stamp their hand on a white piece of construction paper at least 3 times! Have them use a thin brush and green washable paint to create flower stems and leaves!	Sensory Bin Fill your bin with the following: -colorful craft feathers	Shape Spray! Using side walk chalk create a triangle, rectangle, pentagon, and circle. Give your child a spray bottle full of water. Have them identify each shape and then spray it with water!	Bristle Blocks Patterns! Create some fun color patterns using bristle blocks!	Purple Flower Handprints! -washable purple paint -washable green paint -thin brush Sensory Bin: -bin large enough to fit 3 pairs of shoes -colorful craft feathers Shape Spray! Side Walk Chalk Bristle Block Patterns! -bristle blocks

Farm Theme Week: 4

	Circle Time	Craft	Sensory	Gross Motor	Fine Motor	Materials Needed
Monday	Sight Word SAT

Number of the Week :32

Color of the week: Green

Emotion of the Week: Shy

Shape Review Arrow

Your Choice Book! | Shy Little Lady Bug Craft!

Draw a hand sized oval on a green sheet of paper (This is your leaf).

Have your child use kid friendly scissors to cut out the oval.

Have them dip their index finger into some black washable paint. Have them dip their thumb into some red washable paint.

Have them place their two prints together. One of each color next to each other.

Have they take a thin | Sensory Bin

Fill your bin with the following:

- multicolor buttons

-3 different sized plastic Bowls | Energy Burn!

Turn on some fun fast fun background music as you and your child burn some energy!

Skip Across the Room

Hop Back to the start line

Lunge Across the room

Tippy Toe back to the other side!

Repeat 3 Times

Safety First! Always make sure that your child is comfortable doing the activity and that they are hydrated! | Farm Themed age appropriate puzzles! | Shy Little Lady Bug Craft!
-green Construction Paper
-child friendly scissors
-red and black washable finger-paint
-thin brush

Sensory Bin
-plastic Bin large enough to fit 3 pairs of shoes
-multicolor buttons
-3 different sized plastic bowls

Farm Themed age appropriate puzzles

Energy Burn
-fun Back Ground music
-Just Yourselves! |

		brush and black washable paint to create mini sized dots on the lady bugs back (the red print)! When the paint dries Have your child fold the leaf in half so that the lady bug is hiding! As they are working have your child describe a time when they felt shy.				
Tuesday	Sight Word SAT Number of the Week: 32 Color of the week: Green Emotion of the Week: Shy	Triangle Goat Craft! Using a white construction paper cut out a hand sized triangle Using brown construction paper, cut out two mini triangles for the horns	Sensory Bin Fill your bin with the following: -water -green limes -3 different sized plastic cups	Play a Fun Game of guess what I am doing! EX) -climbing a ladder -swimming -paddling a boat -driving a car -hammering	Lace A Necklace! Give your child some yarn and a bowl full of dry rigatoni pasta. Have them lace 32 noodles to create a necklace. When they are done lacing help them to tie the ends of	Triangle Goat -brown, white, and green construction paper -scissors -glue -black washable paint -thin brush -googly eyes Sensory Bin: -plastic Bin large enough to fit 3 pairs of shoes -green limes -water -different sized plastic cups (3)

	Shape Review Arrow Your Choice Book!	Have your child turn the white triangle so that the top of the triangle is facing downward. Have them glue their triangle onto a piece of green construction paper. Have them glue on the mini triangles (these are your horns) Have them glue on two googly eyes Using a thin brush and washable black paint have them dot two nostrils.			the yarn together.	Guess What I'm doing! Take turns guessing what type of activities the other person is pretending to do!
Wednesday	Sight Word: SAT Number of the Week :32 Color of the week:	Tracing Arrows! Using a black marker and yellow construction paper draw 4 different arrows.	Sensory Bin Fill your bin with the following: -clean Soil -plastic toy farm animals	Fun Floor Exercise! Have your child lie on their back and pedal their feet as though they are riding their bike 20 seconds max	Play Dough farm animals! Using play dough have your child mold some fun farm animals!	Tracing Arrows -yellow construction paper -black marker -yarn Sensory Bin: -plastic bin large enough to fit 3 pairs of shoes -clean Soil -plastic toy farm animals

	Green Emotion of the Week: Shy Shape Review Arrow Your Choice Book!	Make them the length of the page. Give your child some precut yarn strands to trace their arrows!	-small plastic toy shovels	Lie down next to them and do the same. Have them turn on their belly and have them pretend swim 20 seconds max Have them sit up and reach for their toes for a good stretch. 20 Repeat 3 Times Safety First! Always check your child to make sure that they are safe, comfy and having fun!		-small plastic toy shovels Fun Floor Exercises: -yoga Mats -Stretchy comfy clothes Note: Safety First. Always check on your child to make sure that they are safe, comfy and having fun. Play Dough Farm Animals -play dough
Thursday	Sight Word: SAT Number of the Week:32	Feathery 32 Craft! Using a white chalk and black construction paper draw a large number 32	Sensory Bin: Fill your bin with the following: -water	Shape Swat! Blow up a 5 Green Balloons! Using a black marker	Circle "SAT" Using a black pen/marker and a regular sheet of print/lined paper write	Feathery 32 Craft! -craft feathers -black construction paper -white chalk -glue Sensory Bin

	Color of the week: Green Emotion of the Week: Shy Shape Review: Arrow Your Choice Book!	it should take up the full page. Give your child some craft feathers. Have them trace the number 32 with glue and feathers	-green food coloring -child friendly pipettes -green apples	draw a different shape on the side of each balloon -arrow -trapezoid -circle -triangle Give your child a ping pong paddle. Throw the balloons in the air and have your child swat them with their paddle to keep them in the air!	the word "SAT" in multiple locations on the paper (at least 10 times) Have your child use a washable green marker to circle each word.	-plastic bin large enough to fit 3 pairs of shoes -water -child friendly pipettes -green food coloring -green apples Shape Swat -ping pong paddle -green balloons -black marker Circle "SAT" -regular sheet of print/lined paper -black marker/pen -green washable marker
Friday	Sight Word: SAT Number of the Week: 32 Color of the week: Green Emotion of the Week:	Goose Craft Precut a yellow triangle using construction paper. It should be half of the size of your index finger (this is the beak). Cover the palm of your child's	Sensory Bin: Fill your bin with the following: -dry oatmeal -plastic funnels -plastic toy farm animals -plastic measuring cups	Play a Game of Animal Charades with your Child! What type of farm animal am I? Fun Ideas: -Gallop Like A horse	ABC Trace Using a black marker or pen, in broken lines write down letters A-Z on a regular sheet of print/lined paper. Make them large	Goose Craft -yellow construction paper -white washable paint -blue construction paper -paint brush -googly eyes -glue Sensory Bin: -plastic bin large enough to fit 3 pairs of shoes -dry oatmeal -plastic funnels

	Shy Shape Review Arrow Your Choice Book!	hand in washable white paint. Have them leave their hand print on a blue sheet of construction paper. Turn the paper so that the finger prints are horizontal (This is the body of the goose. Have your child use a paint brush and washable white paint to draw on the goose neck and a circle for the head. Have your child glue on the triangle for the beak. Have them glue on two googly eyes		-Roll around the carpet like a muddy piglet! -Walk like a Chicken! -Waddle like a duckling!	enough for your child to easily trace them. Have them use their favorite color washable marker to trace.	-plastic toy farm animals -plastic measuring cups Farm Animal Charades: What Type of Farm animal Am I? -just yourselves! ABC Trace -regular sheet print/lined of paper -pen/marker -washable marker

Theme Bugs Week: 1

	Circle Time	Craft	Sensory	Gross Motor	Fine Motor	Materials Needed
Monday	Sight Word: AN Number of the Week :33 Color of the week: White Review Diamond Book of Choice!	Bug painting Using a black marker draw 3 circles One on top of the other on a yellow piece of construction paper. 1Head 2Thorax 3 Abdomen Have your child use washable green paint to trace and fill in each of the circles. Have them use black washable paint and a thin brush to draw on 3 legs on either side of the bug Have them draw on two antennas. As they are working explain to them that	Sensory Bin Fill your bin with the following: -kinetic sand -plastic bug toys	Bug Spray! Using a piece of sidewalk chalk. Draw 4 different bugs (simple just a circle with 6 legs will do.) In the middle of each circle write down a different word 1)AN 2)HAT 3)AT 4)SAT Give each your child a spray bottle filled with water. Have them identify each of the words and then spray them!	Glittering Diamonds Using a black construction paper and a black piece of construction paper Draw 3 diamonds, one inside of the other. The biggest diamond should take up the full page. Have your child use glitter glue to trace the lines of each of the diamonds.	Bug Painting -green and black washable paint -yellow construction paper -black marker Sensory Bin: -plastic bin large enough to fit 3 pairs of shoes -kinetic sand -plastic bug toys Bug Spray -Sidewalk chalk -spray bottle filled with water -If you are doing this activity indoors draw the bugs on a regular sheet of paper. Place the paper over a mat or towel to soak up the water.

		an insect different body parts including: Head, Thorax, Abdomen and Antennas. Insects have 6 legs.				Glittering Diamonds -black construction paper -glitter glue -chalk
Tuesday	Sight Word: AN Number of the Week :33 Color of the week: White Review Diamond Your Choice Book!	Ant Fingerprints! Have your child dip their finger in some brown/red washable paint. Have them press down a green sheet of paper to create 3 fingerprints (the finger prints should be close together to form head, thorax and abdomen. Using a black marker/pen draw on 6 legs Repeat this process at least 6 times around the	Sensory Bin: Fill your bin with the following: -sunflower Seeds -plastic bowls -plastic measuring cups	Fly Swat! Blow up some Balloons. Draw two big bug eyes on them Give your child a clean bug swatter! Toss them in the air and have your child run to swat the flies!	ABC REVIEW Using a pen or marker write down letters Aa-Zz on a regular sheet of print/lined paper. Have your child identify each letter. As they go through the letters have them use their favorite crayon to circle the letters that they have mastered.	Ant Fingerprints! -brown/red washable paint -green construction paper -black marker Sensory Bin: -plastic bin large enough to fit 3 pairs of shoes -sunflower seeds -plastic bowls -plastic measuring cups Always supervise your child when working with small objects that may pose choking hazard.

		paper, so that it looks like ants walking around grass.				Fly Swat -Balloons -Clean Fly Swatter ABC REVIEW -regular sheet of print/lined paper -crayon -marker/pen
Wednesday	Sight Word: AN Number of the Week: 33 Color of the week: White Review Diamond Your Choice Book!	Napkin Butterflies! Give your child some paper napkins. Have them dip their fingers in some washable finger-paints (color of their choice). Have them decorate both sides of their napkins (5 napkins total). When they are done tie a rubber band around the middle of each of the napkins so that they look like butterflies!	Sensory Bin: Fill your bin with the following: -green -leaves -sticks -grass -clean Soil -plastic toy bugs	Catch the Butterflies. Use the napkin butterflies you made during craft time! Toss the butterflies in the air and have your child run to catch them with their butterfly net!	Bristle Block Bugs! Using bristle blocks build some colorful bugs with your child!	Napkin Butterflies! -paper napkins -washable finger-paints (child's choice colors). -rubber bands Sensory Bin: -plastic bin large enough to fit 3 pairs of shoes -green Leaves -sticks -grass -clean Soil -plastic toy bugs Always supervise your child when playing with small objects that my pose choking hazard.

		You will use this craft for today's gross motor skill activity!				Catch the butterflies! -paper napkins -rubber bands -play butterfly net Bristle Block Bugs! -Bristle Blocks!

Thursday	Sight Word: AN Number of the Week :33 Color of the week: White Review Diamond Your Choice Book!	Square Winged Butterfly On a piece of white construction paper draw a diamond in the center (make it about the size of your hand). On either side of the diamond draw two squares so that the squares are touching the diamond (these are your butterfly wings)	Build Ant Hills! Fill your sensory bin with the following: -kinetic sand -plastic ants -plastic shovels	Fun Bug Moves! Hop Across the room like a grasshopper Crawl back like an ant! Repeat 3 times! Safety First! Always make sure your child is comfortable doing the activity and that are hydrated.	Sticker Fun! Fold a regular sheet of paper into 6 squares. Using a black pen or marker, write down the following words: AN HAT SAT CAT One word per square! In one of the remaining squares write down the number 33, and draw a	Square Winged butterfly -white construction paper -washable paints (child's choice) -thin paint brush -washable paint dotters (child's choice) Sensory Bin: -kinetic Sand -plastic ants -plastic shovels Fun Bug Moves! Just yourselves! Sticker Fun!

		Have your child trace the diamond and the squares with a thin paint brush and washable paint of their choice. Have them decorate inside of the wings with washable paint dotters.			diamond in the other. Have your child place a sticker on each box that they have mastered.	-any fun stickers will work! -regular sheet of paper -black pen or marker.
Friday	Sight Word: AN Number of the Week: 33 Color of the week: White Review Diamond Your Choice Book!	Cute Little Bee! Precut a black triangle (this is your bee stinger). It should be the size of your ring, middle, and index finger put together. On a yellow construction paper draw a circle (the size of your hand. Draw a circle on either side of the original	Sensory Bag: Use a red, green, and purple marker to draw 3 diamonds on the bag. Fill the bag with clear hair gel. Add greed, red, and purple water beads or some pom poms to the bag. Seal the bag tightly and tape it to the table.	Bee's help flowers grow! Drop of the pollen! Fill a laundry basket with bean bags. Set out 4 different containers around the room. Have your child push their basket of bean bags to each bucket and drop off a bean bag.	Molding Bugs! Give your child some play dough Have them mold some bugs!	Cute Little Bee -yellow construction paper -glue -googly eyes -paint brush -washable black, and white paint -black construction paper. Sensory Bag: -purple, green, and red marker -Ziploc bag -purple green and red water beads or colorful pom poms.

| | | circle (these are your wings)

Have your child use washable back ink to create black lines across the circle to form a yellow/black pattern.

Have them draw on two antennas

Using washable white paint have them trace and fill in the wings.

Have them glue on the triangle stinger to the bottom of the circle.

Have them glue on two googly eyes to their bee. | Have your child maneuver the beads or pom poms to the matching colored diamond. | | | (Always supervise your child when working with small objects that could be choking hazards. Make sure the bag is fully sealed before allowing your child to play).

Drop off the Pollen!

-bean bags
-laundry basket
-4 different baskets/or plastic containers

Molding Bugs!

-play dough |

Bug Theme Week: 2

	Circle Time	Craft	Sensory	Gross Motor	Fine Motor	Materials needed
Monday	Sight Word: CAN

Number of the Week :34

Color of the week: Black

Review Rectangle

Your Choice Book! | Caterpillar Craft!

Give your child a paper cup.

Set out some green and yellow washable paint.

Have them dip the top of their cup in the washable paints and then stamp the cup onto a white construction paper.

Have them alternate between colors so that they create a green and yellow pattern.

Have them glue on two googly eyes

Give them a washable red marker to draw on a happy face! | Sensory Bin:

Take some plastic straws and cut them into smaller pieces, then drop them in your sensory bin.

Give your child some plastic measuring cups | Busy Bee

Collect the nectar and take it back to the hive!

Set up Different colored bean bags throughout the room (Pretend the bean bags are nectar).

Set an empty container in the middle of the room.

Have your little bee race around collecting all the colored bean bags, and then race to the empty bin to drop them in (pretend the empty container is the hive).

Make sure they collect only one bean bag at a time. | Water color shapes!

Draw a rectangle on a white construction paper

Draw a diamond

Draw a square

Note: All shapes should be the size of your hand.

Give your child some water colors and have them paint each shape with their color of choice. | Caterpillar Craft!
-white construction paper
-yellow and green washable paint
-paper cup
-red washable marker
-googly eyes
-glue

Sensory Bin:
-plastic bin large enough to fit 3 pairs of shoes
-plastic measuring cups

Busy Bee
-multicolored bean bags
-1 empty plastic container (laundry basket).

Water Color Shapes
-water color paints
-paint brush
-white construction paper
-marker to draw shapes |

Tuesday	Sight Word: CAN Number of the Week :34 Color of the week: Black Review Rectangle Your Choice Book!	Shapes and Bugs Craft! Have your child tear some black construction paper into small pieces. Using a black marker and a white construction paper draw a circle towards the top of the paper, then draw another circle directly beneath the first circle, finally, draw a vertical rectangle directly beneath the second circle. All of the shapes should be touching. The first circle is the bug's head, the second circle is the thorax, and the rectangle is the abdomen. Give your child six thin rectangles cut	Sensory Bin Fill your bin with the following: -green -rotini pasta -plastic scoops. (Fill a large Ziploc bag with some dry rotini pasta. Add a few drops of washable green paint. Shake the bag so that the pasta is covered in green paint, then spread the contents out to dry on a mat. When the pasta is dry add it to your sensory bin.	Number Touch! Write down numbers 24-34 on a large butcher paper, then tape it to the wall. Have your child stand across the room from the numbers. Set some washable finger paints next to them. Have them dip their fingers in the color of choice then race to identify and dot the numbers (one at a time!)	Lego Word Review! Using a washable marker write down the following words on some Legos: "can" "an" "hat "at" "sat" One word per Lego. Set them up in front of your child. Have your child identify each word. Have them create a tower of the words that they have mastered.	Shapes and Bugs Crafts! -black tissue paper -white construction paper -black construction paper -black washable marker -glue Sensory Bin -plastic bin large enough to fit 3 pairs of shoes -dry rotini pasta -washable green paint -plastic scoops Number Touch! -washable finger paints -butcher paper -black marker to write the numbers Lego Word Review -washable marker -Legos

		from black construction paper (bug legs) Have your child glue the torn black paper inside of each of the shapes. Have them glue on the legs 3 legs to each side. Give them a washable marker and have them draw on 2 antennas.				
Wednesda y	Sight Word: CAN Number of the Week: 34 Color of the week: Black Review Rectangl e Your Choice Book!	Fuzzy Caterpillar Craft Give your child a popsicle stick. Have them glue fuzzy pom poms onto the stick to create a fuzzy caterpillar.	Sensory Bin: Fill your bin with the following: -water beads and water bead scoops! ALWAYS supervise your child when working with small objects that may pose	Insect Style Workout! -play some of your child's favorite dance music in the background! Flap your wings as fast as a dragonfly Crawl slowly like quiet lady bug. Jump high like a flea!	Build your Name! Using Lego blocks and a washable marker write down the letters of your child's name. One letter per Lego. Have your child place the Legos together to build their name.	Fuzzy Caterpillar Craft -fuzzy pom poms -glue -popsicle stick Sensory Bin: -water beads -water bead scoops :They look like scissors that come with two mini bowls attach to each side, which will allow your child to scoop up the beads

			choking hazard.			ALWAYS supervise your child when working with small objects
						Insect Style Workout -fun music -just yourselves
						Build Your Name! -Legos -washable marker
Thursday	Sight Word: CAN Number of the Week :34 Color of the week: Black Review Rectangle Your Choice Book!	Caterpillar Transformation Craft! Give your child some brown washable paint, a paintbrush, and a paper cup. Have them paint the outside of the cup brown. Have them dip their finger in some green washable paint and create 3 consecutive dots on the inside of the cup to form a caterpillar. Fold a tissue paper square	Sensory Bin: Ant Picnic Fill your bin with the following: -plastic play food, toy plates and scoops. -Some plastic toy ants	Go outside on a Bug Hunt! Give your child a kid friendly magnifying glass. Have them go on a bug hunt in their own back yard or around the neighborhood. How many bugs can you spot together!	Insect Art! Give your child some washable paints and a white construction paper. Have them paint a picture of their favorite insect!	Caterpillar Transformation Craft -paper cup -brown washable paint -tissue paper -string of yarn. -green washable paint Ant Picnic Sensory Bin: -plastic bin large enough to fit 3 pairs of shoes -plastic toy ants -plastic toy food -plastic toy plates -plastic scoops Bug Hunt -child friendly magnifying class.

		in half and tie it in the middle with a piece of yarn (This is your butterfly). Place the butterfly into the cup once the caterpillar is dry. Explain to your child how a fuzzy goes into the cocoon (a little house) and comes out as a beautiful butterfly!				Insect Art -washable paints -white construction paper -paint brush
Friday	Sight Word: CAN Number of the Week: 34 Color of the week: Black Review Rectangl e Your choice Book!	Lady Bug Plate Craft! Give your child a paper plate. Give them some red and black washable paint. Have them paint half of the plate red and half of the plate black. Have them glue on two googly eyes to	Sensory Bag -using a black marker draw a rectangle in the middle of the bag. Fill the bag with clear hair gel and water beads (10). Make sure the bag is complete	Run Beekeeper! Have your child pretend he/she is a beekeeper and the bees are after you for taking their honey! Using painter's tape create a zig zag pattern across the floor of your chosen room! Have your child run zig zags to get	Numbers and Patterns Using a black marker write the number 34 on a piece of white constructio n paper. The number should take up at least half of the page. Have your child use a red and black dotter	Lady Bug Plate Craft -paper plate -red and black washable paint -paint brush. -googly eyes -glue Sensory Bag -large zip lock bag -water beads (10) -clear hair gel. -tape (Always supervise your child when they are working with

		the black side of the plate. Have them dip their finger in the black washable paint and dot the red side of the plate.	sealed and tape it to the table. Have your child use their fingers to maneuver all of the water beads into the rectangle.	away from the bees! Play a recording of Flight of the Bumble Bee by Nikolai Rimsky-Korsakov to make it more fun!	to trace the number. Have them create a red and black pattern of colors as they trace.	small objects. You do not want them to put a water bead in their mouth, nose, or ears!) Run Beekeeper! -painter's tape -audio recording of Flight of the Bumble Bee by Nikolai Rimsky-Korsakov Numbers and Patterns -black marker -White Construction paper -red and black washable paint dotters

Bug Theme Week: 3

	Circle Time	Craft	Sensory	Gross Motor	Fine Motor	Materials Needed
Monday	Sight Word: RAN

Number of the Week:35

Color of the week: Yellow

Review Triangle

Your Choice Book! | Yellow Flower Handprints

Cover your child's palm and fingers with washable yellow paint.

Have them leave their hand prints on a piece of white construction paper. Have them use a paint brush and some washable green paint to draw the flower stems and the leaves.

Have them add some drops of gold glitter glue to the center of their flower for some glittery pollen! | Listen and Feel Activity

Have your child close their eyes.

Play a buzzing bee recording for them.

Tickle their arm with a soft feather. Tell them it's a butterfly's wing brushing against them!

Have them listen to a chirping cricket! | The Ants Are Marching!

March around the room with your child! If possible gather a few family members to join in!

Make sure to keep a fast pace and your knees high!

Play the Ants Go Marching by Ananda Sen | Yellow Cotton!

Write down the word "ran" multiple times on a regular sheet of paper (10 times).

Give your child a cotton ball. Have your child dip their cotton ball in some yellow washable paint.

Have them read the word out loud each time before they dot it! | Yellow Flower Handprints -white construction paper -washable yellow paint -paintbrush -green washable paint -gold glitter glue

Feel and Listen Activity -soft Feather -buzzing Bee Recording

The Ants are Marching -The Ants Go Marching song by Ananda Sen

Yellow Cotton -cotton ball -yellow washable paint -regular sheet of paper - pen/marker |

254

					to write down word
Tuesday	Sight Word: RAN Number of the Week :35 Color of the week: Yellow Review Triangle Your Choice Book!	Shoo Fly Craft! Using white construction paper precut two small circles (these are the bug's eyes). They should be no bigger than your index finger. Precut a small triangle (this will be used for wings). It should be no bigger than your index finger. Paint the inside of your child's hand with black washable ink. Have them leave their handprint on a green construction paper. Turn the paper so that the fingers are	Fill a Ziploc bag with some clear hair gel Add some plastic play letters "R" "A" "N" Include other letters as well, just make sure that "R" "A" and "N" are included in the letters. Seal the bag and tape it to the table. Have your child maneuver the letters around with their fingers to spell the word "RAN"	Grasshopper Hop Over! Place 5 pool noodle on the floor. Lay them side by side, but leave enough room for your child to hop over each one. Have your child hop over the pool noodles Tell them that they are grasshoppers hopping over a twigs!	35 Sunflower Seeds On a blue piece of construction paper write down the number 35.It should take up at least half a page. Have your child trace the number with glue. -Give them a bowl filled with sunflower seeds. Have them count 35 seeds and glue them onto the number.	Shoo Fly Craft -green and white construction paper -black washable paint -paint brush -washable black marker Squish Bag -clear hair gel -plastic alphabet letters make sure that the letters "R" "A" "N" are included in your letter selection. 35 Sunflower Seeds -blue construction paper -sunflower seeds -glue -plastic bowl -black marker to write the number 35

					Grass Hopper Hop Over! Pool Noodle
		facing downward. The fingers are the bug's legs. Have your child glue on the two precut circles for the eyes Have them glue on the triangle for the wings. Make sure the triangle is upside down so that the top corner is touching the handprint. Give your child a washable black marker to dot the fly's eyes!			
Wednesday	Sight Word: RAN Number of the Week: 35 Color of the week: Yellow	Butterfly Craft! Give your child a coffee filter, a paintbrush, and some water colors. Have them paint the water filter	Sensory Bin Fill your bin with the following: -pebbles -water -plastic cups Always supervise your child when working	Building Ant Tunnels! Using Chairs and blankets help your child to build an ant tunnel! Have fun pretending you are ants deep inside an ant hill!	Triangle Fun! Give your child 5 pipe cleaners. Have your child bend the pipe cleaners to create triangles shapes.	Butterfly Craft! -coffee Filter -watercolors -paintbrush -glue -clothespin Sensory Bin: -plastic bin large enough to

		with the colors of their choice. Set it out to dry! Then have them fold the filter in half and glue it onto a clothespin! The coffee filter is the butterfly wings and the clothespin is the body!	with small objects that may pose choking hazard!			fit 3 pairs of shoes -pebbles -water -plastic cups Always supervise your child when working with small objects that may pose choking hazard! Building Ant Tunnels! -chairs -blankets Makes sure everything is secure. Always remember safety first! Triangle Fun -pipe cleaners
	Review Triangle Your Choice Book!					
Thursday	Sight Word: RAN Number of the Week: 35 Color of the week: Yellow	Dragonfly Craft -precut white tissue paper squares Glue 2 pipe cleaners onto a piece of black construction	Sensory Bin Fill your bin with the following: -plastic ABC letters -kinetic sand	Over Under: Crawl under the leaves like a lady bug, and hop over the rocks like a grasshopper! Set up pool noodle	Dot number 35 Using a chalk board and white chalk write down the number 35 multiple times (at least 10 times.)	Dragon Fly Craft -white tissue paper -white chalk -black construction paper -pipe cleaners -glue

	Review Triangle	paper. Place them directly next to each other. Using a white chalk draw 4 rectangles 2 on either side of the pipe cleaners (These are the wings) Have your child glue on precut white tissue paper squares so that the rectangles are fully covered.		obstacle course. Place two buckets on the ground. Place one end of a pool noodle in each bucket so that it stands up to create a hoop! You might have to fill it with bean bags or small pillows to keep it from falling down. Place a large pillow on the floor. Then set up another 2 buckets and a second noodle as a hoop. Then place a second pillow on the floor. Then place a third pillow, and a third hoop! Have your child hop over the	Scatter the number around the board. Give your child some wet Q-tips. Have them use the Q- Tip to dot each number 35.	-Sensory Bin: -plastic bin large enough to fit 3 pairs of shoes -kinetic sand -ABC letters Over and Under -6 pool noodles -6 buckets -bean bag/pillow fillers -3 pillows Dot 35 -chalkboard -white chalk -Q-tips -water

				pillows, and craw under the hoops!		
Friday	Sight Word: RAN

Number of the Week :35

Color of the week: Yellow

Review Triangle

Your Choice Book! | Firefly Craft

Give your child an empty roll of toilet paper. Have them dip their roll into some washable black paint.

Have them create 5 different circles throughout a blue construction paper.

Have them fill in each circle with a yellow dotter.

Have them dip their finger in some black washable paint. Next have them create a finger print next to each circle (make sure the fingerprint touches the circle.

Have them glue on two | Sensory Bin:

Fill your bin with some glow in the dark sticks Take your bin into a dimly lit room and have your child play with some pretend fireflies! | Glow Bug Tag!

Play a game of Tag in your backyard after the sun goes down! Wear some glow in the dark necklace rings! | Word Review

Using any color dry erase marker, write down the word "RAN" in different areas of the white board. Have your child use a dry erase marker of their choice to circle each word. Make sure they read the word out loud as they are circling it. | Firefly Craft
-empty toilet paper roll
-yellow dotters
-black washable paint
-googly eyes
-glue
-blue construction paper

Sensory Bin:
-plastic bin large enough to fit 3 pairs of shoes
-glow sticks

Glow Bug Tag
-glow in the dark necklace Rings

Safety First! Always make sure your play area is safe and free of any tripping hazards!

Word Review
-dry erase board
-dry erase markers |

		googly eyes to each fingerprint.				

Bug Theme Week: 4

	Circle Time	Craft	Sensory	Gross Motor	Fine Motor	Materials Needed
Monday	Sight Word: IS

Number of the Week :36

Color of the week: Pink

Shape Review: Square

Your Choice Book! | Flower Craft!

Precut an oval using green construction paper (This will be your leaf.)

Flower Craft Give your child a green pipe cleaner.

Give them a coffee filter.

Have them dip their finger in some washable pink paint and then dot around the coffee filter (tell them that they are decorating their flower petals)

Have them glue on some yellow fuzzy pom poms to the center of coffee filter | Sensory Bin

Fill your bin with the following:

-water
-red ice

Mix some water with red food coloring. Fill up some ice cube trays and freeze them. When the red cubes are frozen add them to your bin.

-plastic soup spoon and plastic bowls. | Use Your Feet!

Have your child sit on the floor.

Blow up 5 balloons.

Have them transfer the balloons from one side to the other by holding the balloons between their feet! | Glittering Shapes!

Using a washable black marker, draw a square, circle, and a triangle on a pink construction paper.

Give your child some glitter glue.

Have them trace the lines of each shape with the glue.

Have them glue on some googly eyes and then use a washable red marker to draw a happy smile to teach face. | Flower Craft
-green construction paper
-coffee filter
-yellow pomp oms
-green pipe cleaner

Sensory Bin:
-plastic bin large enough to fit 3 pairs of shoes
-water
-ice trays
-red food coloring

-plastic soup spoon
-plastic bowls

Use Your Feet!
-balloons (5).

Glittering Shapes:
-glitter glue
-pink construction paper
-googly eyes
-washable red marker
-glue |

		(this is pollen). Have them glue on the precut oval to pipe cleaner (This is your leaf). Finally glue the coffee filter onto the pipe cleaner.				
Tuesday	Sight Word: IS Number of the Week :36 Color of the week: Pink Shape Review: Square Your Choice Book!	Pink Square Craft On a piece of white construction paper draw a large square The square should take up most of the paper. Have your child trace the square with some pink glitter glue! Give your child some precut pink tissue paper squares. Have them glue the tissue paper	Sensory Bin Fill your bin with the following: -dry colorful cereal ex(Fruit Loops Plastic measuring cups	Word Wall Balls! Using a black marker write down the following words on sheets of regular print paper. IS AN AT (one word per paper) Make sure the words are large enough for your child to	Buttons! Buttons! Buttons! Give your child a clothing item that has multiple buttons. (preferably large buttons) Have them practice buttoning and unbuttoning the shirt/sweater/coat	Pink Square Craft -pink tissue paper -white construction paper -pink glitter glue Sensory Bin: -plastic bin large enough to fit 3 pairs of shoes -colorful cereal ex) fruit loops -plastic measuring cups Word Wall Balls -regular paper -tape -bouncy ball

		to the inside area of the square. The entire area should be covered.		see from a distance. Tape them to the wall. Give your child a bouncy ball Have your child play a game of word wall balls! Have them identify each word before they bounce the ball off the word!		-black marker Buttons! Buttons! Buttons! Clothing items that have buttons. Large buttons work best!
Wednesday	Sight Word: IS Number of the Week :36 Color of the week: Pink Shape Review: Square Your Choice Book!	Glow Bugs and Flower Craft! Have your child dip a dishwashing brush into some washable pink paint. Have them stamp their brush onto a black piece of construction paper (these are your flowers).	Sensory Bin: Fill your bin with the following: -dry pink rice (Fill a large Ziploc bag with some rice and add a few drops of washable pink paint. Seal the bag and mix the	Take some time to stretch! Play some fun relaxing fun music in the background! Feel Free to join your child for a fun a calming stretch session. From a sitting position reach for your toes!	Pipe cleaner Bugs! Help your child twists some pipe cleaners together to create some bugs!	Glow Bug and Flower Craft! -washable pink, yellow and green paint -black construction paper -thin paint brush -clean dishwashing brush -Sensory Bin: -plastic bin large enough to fit 3 pairs of shoes

		Using a thin paint brush and some washable green paint have them create some stems for their flowers. Have them dip their finger in some washable yellow paint and dot around the rest of the paper (these are your glow bugs).	contents of the bag so that the rice if fully covered. Spread the contents of the bag out to dry on a plastic mat. When the rice is dry place it in your sensory bin.) -plastic funnels -plastic measuring cups	Stand up on your tippy toes and touch the sky. Lie Down and bring your knees to your chest. Lie flat at just breath. Remember Safety first! Do not over stretch or push your child to strain themselves		-pink rice(pink washable paint, zip lock bag, mat) -plastic funnels -plastic measuring cups Pipe cleaner bugs! -pipe cleaners Take a moment to stretch! Just Yourselves and some relaxing background music! Remember Safety first! Do not over stretch or push your child to strain themselves.
Thursday	Sight Word: IS Number of the Week :36	Stick Insect Craft 7 popsicle sticks Using a black marker and a green	Sensory Bin: Fill your bin with the following: -water	5/10/15 Join your child for a fun workout!	Buttons and Zippers! Give your child some of their clothes that have buttons and zippers on them.	Stick Insect Craft -7 popsicle sticks -black marker -green construction paper

| | Color of the week: Pink

Shape Review: Square

Your Choice Book! | construction paper as a base draw a vertical line.

Draw 3 horizontal lines on each side of the vertical line.

Have your child glue the popsicle sticks to each of the lines.

Have them use a washable brown marker to draw two antennas to the top of the bug! | -purple food coloring
-flower petals (fake or real)
-bath bubbles

- | Run in place for 5 Seconds

Place a pool noodle on the floor.

Have your child hop over the pool noodle 10 Times

Finish with 15Mountain Climbers

Safety First! Make sure your child is comfortable doing the workout. Make sure that they are not overexerting themselves. Take breaks and have fun! Always hydrate! | Have them practice zipping, and buttoning up clothes. | -glue
-brown washable marker

Sensory Bin:
-plastic bin large enough to fit 3 pairs of shoes
-water
-bath bubbles
-purple food coloring
-flower petals (fake or real)

5/10/15

-fun workout music
-yourselves

SAFETY FIRST:
Make sure your child is comfortable and does not over exert themselves. This is meant to be a fun energy burner. Make sure to stay hydrated. Take breaks if you need to or modify. |

						Buttons and Zippers -Clothing items that have buttons and zippers. They do not have to wear them just practice buttoning and zipping. For zippers I would work with easy plastic zippers not the metal kind.
Friday	Sight Word: IS Number of the Week :36 Color of the week: Pink Shape Review: Square	Honeybee Handprint Paint the inside of your child's hand with washable yellow paint. Have them leave their yellow handprint on a white construction paper. Have them use a thin paint brush and washable black paint to draw	Sensory Bin Fill your bin with the following: -water beads -water bead scoops -plastic toy bugs Always supervise your child when working with small objects that might pose a	ABC Catch! Play a Game of Catch with a big bouncy Ball! As you are playing sing your ABC song!	36 Pink Dots! Using a black marker and white construction paper write down numbers 1-36. Have your child dip their finger in some washable pink paint. Have them count out loud as they dot each number with their finger.	Honeybee handprint -white construction paper -black and yellow washable paint -thin brush Sensory Bin: -water beads -water bead scoops -plastic toy bugs 36 Paint Dots -pink washable finger-paint

| | | horizontal lines across their hand print.

Have them draw 2 antennas.

Have them glue on two googly eyes. | choking hazard! | | | -white construction paper
-black marker

ABC Catch!
-Big Bouncy Ball |

Ocean Theme Week: 1

	Circle Time	Craft	Sensory	Gross Motor	Fine Motor	Materials Needed
Monday	Sight Word: HIS Number of the Week: 37 Color of the week: Orange Review Trapezoid Your Choice Book!	Handprint fish! Paint the inside of your child's hand with orange washable paint. Have them leave their handprint on a blue construction paper. Have them dip the end of an empty roll of toilet paper in some white washable paint, and then press it onto the paper. The circles will be the air bubbles! When the paint dries have them glue on two googly eyes Have your child use some washable black paint	Sensory Bin Fill your bin with the following: -water -ocean themed plastic toys (sharks, fish, whales etc.) -fish bowl gravel Always supervise your child when playing with small items, which may cause choking hazard!	Beach Volley Ball Using painter's tape create a line in the middle of the room (pretend it's a net). Play a fun game of volley using a balloon!	37 Fish Scales Give your child a paper plate. Precut a trapezoid fish tail using green construction paper the size of your hand. Using a black marker, write down numbers 1-37 on the plate. Give your child a celery stick. Have your child dip the end of their stick in some green washable paint. Have them count and identify each number as they stamp the painted end of the	Handprint Fish -white, black and orange washable paint -blue construction paper -empty toilet paper roll -thin brush Sensory Bin: -plastic bin large enough to fit 3 pairs of shoes -water -fish bowl gravel -ocean themed plastic toys Always supervise your child when playing with small objects that may pose choking hazard. Beach Volley Ball! -Balloon -painter's tape 37 Fish Scales -paper plate -green washable paint -green construction paper -glue -googly eyes -black marker

		with a thin brush to draw on some scales on their fish!			celery on each numbers to create fish scales. When they are done glue on two googly eyes and the construction paper trapezoid tail!	
Tuesday	Sight Word: HIS Number of the Week :37 Color of the week: Orange Review Trapezoid Your Choice Book!	Oyster Pearl Craft! Give your child two paper plates. Have them use a thin paint brush and black washable paint to draw lines across the backside of the first plate. This is the top of your oyster Using a regular paint brush and pink washable paint have them cover the inside area of the second plate.	Sensory Bin: Fill your bin with the following: -sand -sand castle building materials ex)small plastic shovel, small rake, and plastic cups	Play a game of Frisbee! It may be hard for your child to catch a Frisbee so gage their ability. If they are not ready to catch show them how to throw a Frisbee! Have fun!	Colorful Corals! Give your child some pipe cleaners! Have them twist together some colorful corals!	Oyster Pearl Craft -2 white paper plates -black and pink washable paint -Styrofoam ball (hand size) -2 paint brushes (one should be a thin brush) -hole puncher -yarn Sensory Bin: -plastic bin large enough to fit 3 pairs of shoes -sand -sand castle building materials ex) small rake, small plastic cups, plastic shovel etc. Frisbee Game -child friendly Frisbee! Colorful Corals! -multicolor pipe cleaners

		When the paint has dried place both plates together. One on top of the other to form the oyster. Use a hole puncher to punch two holes on each plate. Make sure they perfectly lined up. Lace some white yarn through the holes, and tie the plates together.

Finally, glue a white Styrofoam ball in the center of the bottom plate. (That is your pearl).

. | | | | |
| Wednesday | Sight Word: HIS | Shark's Mouth! | Sensory Bottle: | Pretend Diving! | Goldfish Snack Reading! | Shark's Mouth -1 paper plate |

	Number of the Week:37 Color of the week: Orange Review Trapezoid Your Choice Book!	Precut a grey triangle (the size of your palm) This is your shark Fin! Cut mini triangles using a white construction paper (shark teeth) Give your child a paper plate, red washable paint, and a paint brush. Have them cover the inside of the plate in red paint. After the inside of the plate dries have them use grey washable paint to cover the entire back area of the plate. The plate should be red on the inside and	Fill a plastic bottle with some sand (half way), Throw in some sea shells. Seal it tightly before you give it to your child.	Give your child some swim goggles! Grab some for yourself as well! Place a towel/mat on the floor. Place different pretend fish on the floor (bean bags/stuffed animals, pillows etc. Pretend to jump in the water, then lie down on your tummy and pretend to swim around. Turn Around and flutter your feet. -pretend to float! Have Fun!	Using a blue construction paper and a black marker write down the word "his" multiple times in different areas of the paper (at least 10 times). Have your child place some gold fish on each of the words. Make them read the word out loud each time. When they are done feel free to enjoy a goldfish snack!	-white and grey construction paper -black, red, and grey washable paint -paint brush Sensory Bottle: -plastic water bottle -sand -plastic seashells Pretend Diving -swim goggles -towel/mat -pretend fish (stuffed animals/pillows/bean bags Goldfish Snack Reading -Blue construction paper -black marker -goldfish snack

| | | grey on the outside.

Fold the paper in half. The red side is the mouth side!

Have your child line the mouth of the shark with glue and then place the white triangles on the glue. Only the bottom part of the triangle should be glued on.

Fold the bottom so that the teeth stand up.

Have your child use washable black paint to dot two shark eyes.

Have them fold the bottom of the grey construction paper triangle and glue it onto | | | | |
|---|---|---|---|---|---|---|

		the top of the plate (Shark Fin).				
Thursday	Sight Word: HIS Number of the Week: 37 Color of the week: Orange Review Trapezoid Your Choice Book1	Sea Turtle Craft Precut 4 ovals using green construction paper. These are the turtle flippers. They should be no bigger than 2 fingers) Precut a circle using green construction paper. It should be about half the size of your palm. Give your child a paper plate bowl. This will be the turtle shell! Give them some precut some blue tissue paper squares. Have them glue on the	Sensory Bin Fill your bin with the following: -water -blue food coloring -ocean themed plastic toys ex) fish, sharks whales, crabs	Pretend Surfing! Place a mat on the floor Play some fun surf sounds! Place two towels or mats on the floor! Go Pretend Surfing with your child!	Practice Folding! Give your child some towels! Have them practice folding their pretend beach towel!	Sea Turtle Craft -blue tissue paper -green construction paper -glue -paper bowl Sensory Bin: -plastic bin large enough to fit 3 pairs of shoes -ocean themed plastic toys ex) whales, sharks, crabs, fish etc. -water -blue food coloring Pretend Surfing -Some fun ocean surf sound recording -towel/mat Practice Folding -kid sized towels!

		squares so that they completely cover the outside of the bowl. Have them glue the green ovals. (2 ovals on either side of the bowl). Have them glue on the circle for the head!				
Friday	Sight Word: HIS Number of the Week: 37 Color of the week: Orange Review Trapezoid Your Choice Book!	Octopus Arms! Give your child a lunch sized paper bag! Give them some orange washable paint! Have them cover the entire bag in orange paint! After the paint dries, draw 4 vertical lines. They should reach from the middle	What do you hear? Have your child close their eyes! Play some ocean sounds for them! -whale splashing -seagulls -waves crashing	Pretend Kayaking! Have your child sit on a chair! Give them a light broom stick. Have them hold the broom stick over the lap and paddle! Pretend they are in the ocean kayaking! Play some ocean sounds in the background!	Shape Patterns Using geometric tiles have your child create an alternating pattern of trapezoids and squares.	Octopus arms! -lunch size paper bag. -orange and purple washable paint -googly eyes -glue -paint brush - child friendly scissors -black washable marker Ocean Sounds! -Audio recording of whales, ocean waves crashing, seagulls, etc. Pretend Kayaking! -chair! -light stick broom! -ocean sounds! Shape Patterns -geometric tiles

| | | of the bag to the bottom. Use a black washable marker to draw the lines.

Have your child cut along each of the lines. This will create 8 octopus arms!

Have them glue on two googly eyes to the bag.

Have them dip their finger in some purple washable paint and dot tentacles along each of the arms! | | | | Always supervise your child when working with small objects that may pose choking hazard! |
|---|---|---|---|---|---|---|

Ocean Theme Week: 2

	Circle Time	Craft	Sensory	Gross Motor	Fine Motor	Materials Needed
Monday	Sight Word: TO Number of the Week :38 Color of the week: Black Review Hexagon Your Choice Book!	Sail Boat craft! Using a brown construction paper cut out a trapezoid shape. It should be about the size of your hand. Cut out a triangle the size of your hand using a white construction paper (This is your sail). Give your child a popsicle stick, have them glue the top of stick to the center of the triangle. Add the trapezoid to the bottom of the stick!	Sensory Bin: Fill your bin with the following: -blue water beads -plastic scoops -marine life plastic toys ex) whales, sharks, fish, starfish, seahorses etc. Always supervise your child when playing with small objects, which may pose choking hazard.	Gross Motor Skills! Fill up a kiddie pool or the bathtub with some water! Go for a swim! ALWAYS SUPERVISE your child when playing in or around water.	Counting Fish Bait! Give your child a plastic bowl full of gummy worms! Have them use child friendly tweezers to transfer the worms from one bowl to another. Make sure that they count the worms as they transfer them to the empty bowl.	Sail Boat Craft! -white and brown construction paper -popsicle stick -glue Sensory Bin: -plastic bin large enough to fit 3 pairs of shoes -water beads -plastic scoops -marine life plastic toys ex) sharks, whales, starfish, seahorses, etc. ALWAYS SUPERVISE your child when playing with small objects! You do not want them to swallow a water bead! Or to stick one up their nose! Splish Splash Fun! Kiddie Pool/Bathtub

| | | | | | | Never Leave your child unattended in or around water.

Counting Fish Bait
-Gummy Worms
-2 plastic bowls
-child friendly tweezers |
|---|---|---|---|---|---|---|
| Tuesday | Sight Word: TO

Number of the Week :38

Color of the week: Black

Review Hexagon

Your choice Book! | Crab Hand prints!

Paint the inside of your child's hands with red washable paint.

Have your Child press their hands on yellow construction paper. One hand at a time.

Have them press their second handprint down so that the thumb overlaps with the first handprint. | Sea Foam Word Review!

Place a plastic Mat on the table.

Add a glob of shaving cream and drop of washable green paint!

Have your child mix them together for some messy green fun!

Have them practice writing their sight words with their fingers! | Get the Beach Sand Off the towel!

-play a recording of beach waves crashing in the background!

Roll up some beach towels!

Have your child raise their arms over their head and then bring them down while holding the towels

Have them do it multiple times as | Seashell Word Match!

Fold a regular sheet of paper so that when it opens up it has 6 squares.

Write down the following words:

AT
HAT
IS
TO
HIS
CAT

One word per square.

On some note cards write down | Crab Handprints!
-red and black washable paint
-yellow construction paper
-glue
-googly eyes
-thin paint brush

Sea Foam Word Review!
-shaving cream
-green washable paint
-plastic mat

Shake of the Beach Towel!
-3 Rolled up child beach towels |

				though they are shaking of the sand off from a day of beach fun!	the same words (one word per notecard. Give the cards to your child. Have them match the word on the card. As they match the word have them leave a seashell on the box.	-audio recording of ocean waves crashing Seashell Word Match -6 notecards -1 regular sheet of paper -pasta seashells Always supervise your child when playing with small objects.
Have them glue on 2 googly eyes. Have them use a thin brush and black paint to draw on a smile!						
Wednesday	Sight Word: TO Number of the Week: 38 Color of the week: Black Review Hexagon Your Choice Book!	Starfish Craft! On a yellow construction paper draw a large star. The star should take up at least half of the paper. Have your child trace the star with glue. Add some sand to the paper and let it sit for a while. Then carefully tilt paper into a	Ocean Waves Fill a plastic water bottle with some water about half way full! Add a drop of blue food coloring. Add a drop of dish soap Seal the bottle tightly. Turn the bottle to	Ay! Ay ! Captain! Set two chairs together! Give your child a paper plate! Have them pretend that they are the captain of the boat They must maneuver the boat to safety! Play an audio recording of	Tracing Seaweed! Using a black marker, on a blue construction paper draw 3 vertical lines and 3 zig zag lines. Make sure that you alternate between the types of lines. (Lines should touch both ends of the paper.)	Starfish Craft -yellow construction paper -glue -sand -orange washable finger-paint. Sensory Bottle: Ocean Waves and Seafoam -plastic bottle -water -blue food coloring -dish soap Ay! Ay! Captain! -2 chairs

| | | bowl to catch the sand.

Next have your child dip their finger into some orange paint and dot the inside of each of the star arms! | the side and have your child shake the bottle while still holding it horizontal.

Watch them create some waves and sea foam! | an ocean storm.

Sit together and pretend that you are sailing through some rough seas!

Jump up and sit back down as the waves bump the boat!

Sway side to side!

Have Fun! | Give your child some green washable paint and a paint brush.

Have them trace the lines to create some seaweed! | -paper plate
-audio recording of ocean storm

-Tracing Seaweed!

-blue construction paper
-green washable paint
-paint brush
-black marker. |
|---|---|---|---|---|---|---|
| Thursday | Sight Word: TO

Number of the Week :38

Color of the week: Black

Review Hexagon

Your Choice Book! | Ocean Art Give your child a white construction paper.

Add a few drops of blue and white washable paint directly onto the paper.

Give your child a piece of aluminum foil that has been rolled up into a smooth ball | How does it feel?

Fill a tray with some sand

Fill a second tray with water

Fill a tray with some store bought seashells.

Have your child touch the sand. | Beach Ball Fun!

Blow up a beach ball!

Have fun catching and throwing the beach ball with your child! | Fingerprint Counting!

Using a black marker and blue construction paper, write down numbers 1-38.

Have your child dip their finger into some washable black paint.

Have them dot each number as they count 1-38 | Ocean Art
-white construction paper
-washable blue and white paint
-aluminum foil

How does it feel?
-3 trays
-sand
-water
-store bought seashells

Always supervise your child when playing with small objects that |

		the size of your palm. Have your child use the aluminum foil ball to spread the blue and white paint around the paper until it is completely covered.	Have your child dip their hands in the water Have your child feel the seashells with their fingers. Ask them to describe how the contents of each tray feels.			may pose choking hazard. Beach Ball Fun! -Beach ball Fingerprint Counting -blue construction paper -black washable paint -black marker
Friday	Sight Word: TO Number of the Week :38 Color of the week: Black Review Hexagon Your Choice Book!	Jelly Fish Craft Punch holes around the rim of a paper bowl 5-10. Give it to your child. Have them paint the bowl with washable purple paint. Give them precut pink strings of yarn (Enough to thread each of the holes One string per hole. These are	Sensory Bin Fill your bin with the following: -water -seashells Always supervise your child when playing with small objects that may pose a choking hazard!	Sea Creature Sounds! Have your child listen to an audio recording of dolphin, seal, and whale sounds!	Tracing Shapes with Seashells! Using a black marker draw a hexagon on a blue piece of construction paper. The shape should be at least half the size of the paper. Give your child some glue and some dry pasta shells. Have them trace the lines of the hexagon	Jelly Fish Craft -paper bowl -hole puncher -pink yarn -purple washable paint -paintbrush Sensory Bin: Bin large enough to fit 3 pairs of shoes -water -store bought seashells Always supervise your child when playing with small objects that may pose a

		the tentacles)			with the glue and shells!	choking hazard. Sea Creature Sounds! -audio recording of whales, seals, and dolphins, Tracing Shapes with Seashells! -black marker -blue construction paper -dry pasta shells -glue

Ocean Theme Week: 3

	Circle Time	Craft	Sensory	Gross Motor	Fine Motor	Materials Needed
Monday	Sight Word: THE

Number of the Week :39

Color of the week: RED

Review Octagon

Your Choice Book! | Sea Floor Craft

Give your child a paper plate.

Have them use a paint brush and washable blue paint to cover the top half of the plate blue.

Give them brown washable paint and have them paint the bottom half of the plate brown.

Once both sides of the plate are dry, give them some green washable paint and have them draw some vertical lines (sea kelp)

Have them glue on some dry shell pasta | Sensory Bin

Fill your bin with the following:

dry pasta sea shells

-plastic measuring cups | Ocean Clean Up!

Give your child a trash bag.

Go outside and scatter some of the following items on the ground: plastic cups, paper some plastic wraps the kind that holds together sodas or water bottles.

Have your child walk around collecting them.

Explain to them that it is important to keep our oceans clean so that the sea creatures do not eat or get caught in the plastic. | Free the Ocean Creatures!

Using a rubber band tie up some fun plastic marine life toys.

Have your child use their fingers to free them. | Sea Floor Craft:
-paper plate
-washable blue, brown, and green paint
-paint brush
-dry shell pasta
-glue

Sensory Bin:
-plastic bin large enough to fit 3 pairs of shoes
-dry pasta
-plastic measuring cups

Always supervise your child when playing with small objects that may pose choking hazard!

-Ocean Floor Clean Up
-trash bag
-plastic items :

Rings: the kind that hold bottles together
-bottles |

		to the sea floor.				Note: Make sure the tops are off or safely sealed on to the bottle. Always supervise your child when playing with small objects. Also do not leave your child unattended with a plastic bag. They could suffocate if they put it over their head! Safety First!
Tuesday	Sight Word: THE Number of the Week: 39 Color of the week: RED Review Octagon Your Choice Book!	Red and White Fish Craft! Paint the inside of your child's hand using red and white washable paint. Alternate to create a red and white pattern. Have them leave their handprint on some	Sensory Bag: Using a black marker draw the following shapes onto a Ziploc bag: octagon pentagon trapezoid Fill the bag with clear hair gel.	Pretend Roller blading! Put on a helmet knee and arm pads! Finally put on some socks and find a smooth floor area! The socks will make it easy to slide around!	Painting Seashells! Give your child some washable paints, a paint brush, and some store bought shells. Have them paint the shells with the colors of their choice.	Red and White Fish Craft -red and white washable paint -paint brush -blue construction paper -googly eyes -glue Sensory Bag: -black marker -water beads -clear hair gel -Ziploc bag

		blue construction paper. Have them glue on two googly eyes. Have them dip their brush in some white washable paint to draw on some bubbles around the fish!	Add some water beads (6) Have your child maneuver the water beads into each of the shapes. Have your child identify each shape.	Have your child slide their feet from side to side as they make their way around the room. Do it with them. Have fun pretend rollerblading around the room. (Safety first! Make sure that your child is comfortable moving about.) Play some fun beach music in the background!		Pretend Rollerblading -helmet -kneepads -elbow pads -socks -beach theme music Painting Seashells -washable paint -paint brush -store bought shells (5-10) ALWAYS SUPERVISE your child when playing with small items that may pose choking hazard.
Wednesday	Sight Word: THE Number of the Week: 39 Color of the week: RED Review Octagon Your Choice Book!	Fun with Fish Scales! Blow up an orange balloon. Give your child some precut orange tissue paper squares. Have them glue the tissue squares	Sensory Bin Fill you bin with the following: -water -some romaine lettuce leaves (pretend kelp) -some rocks or pebbles	Water Fun with the word "THE" Using side walk chalk write down the word "THE" multiple times on the floor. Have your child use a water hose to erase	Domino Wave! Help your child to set up some dominoes. Stand them up one next to the other. When they are all set up have your child give the first	Fun with Fish Scales! -orange balloon -orange tissue paper -glue -black washable marker Sensory Bin -plastic bin large enough to fit 3 pairs of shoes -rocks

		around their balloon. These are the fish scales! Give them a washable black marker, have them draw on two fish eyes, and a happy smile!	-plastic cups Always supervise your child when playing with small objects that may pose choking hazard!	each one of the words. As they spray water on the word have your child read it out loud!	domino a push! Have fun watching the wave of dominoes!	-romaine lettuce leaves -plastic cups Water Fun with the word "THE" -sidewalk chalk -watering hose Domino Wave -Dominoes
Thursday	Sight Word: THE Number of the Week :39 Color of the week: RED Review Octagon Your choice Book!	Whale Craft Precut a trapezoid the size of your hand using blue construction paper Give your child a paper lunch bag, and some washable blue paint. Have your child use a paint brush to paint both sides of the bag blue. When the paint is dry have your child stuff	Walk on the Sand Roll out a large plastic mat. Spread some sand on the mat Have your child walk on the sand!	Shark Race! Set up a bin across the lawn. Fill it with a few bean bags! Pretend you and your child are two sharks racing for a tasty meal! Race across the yard grab a pretend sea lion (a bean bag) and race back to the start line! See who can make it across the yard/room	Cheerio Trace! Give your child a bowl full of cheerios Write down the number 39 on sheet of red construction paper. The number should take up the full sheet! Have your child trace the lines of the number with glue and then glue on 39 cheerios!	Whale Craft -lunch paper bag -blue washable paint -paintbrush -newspaper -rubber band -glue -blue construction paper -googly eyes Walk on the Sand! -large plastic mat -sand Shark Race! -plastic bin -bean bags Cheerio Trace! -plastic bowl -cheerios

Day						
		the lunch bag with some newspaper. When they are done tie the opening with a rubber band. Have them glue on the trapezoid whale tail to the tied opening! Have your child add two googly eyes!		and back first! Ready Set Go!		-glue -red construction paper -marker to draw number
Friday	Sight Word: THE Number of the Week :39 Color of the week: RED Shape Review: Octagon Your Choice Book!	Octagon Blow Fish On a white piece of construction paper draw a large octagon. The shape should take up at least half of the page! Give your child a plastic fork. Have them dip their fork into some washable	Sensory Bin Fill your bin with the following: -water -bubble bath bubbles -ocean themed bath toys ex) Fish, crabs, whales etc. -dish washing brushes	Give your child a bucket full of water and a bucket full of sponges (5 -10 sponges). Write down the words on the floor using sidewalk chalk: THE IS HIS	Shape Painting! On a piece of white construction use a black marker to draw a circle, an octagon, and a triangle. Give your child a paint brush and some washable red, green, and blue paint.	Octagon Blow Fish -white construction paper -yellow washable paint -plastic fork -glue -googly eyes Sensory Bin: Plastic bin large enough to fit 3 pairs of shoes -bubble bath -ocean themed bath toys ex) whales, fish, crabs, etc.

| | | yellow paint. Have your child stamp their fork inside of the octagon.

Make it so that they cover the entire shape.

Have your child glue on some googly eyes to their blow fish! | | AT

HAT

Have your child soak their sponge the water, then identify one of the words and finally toss the sponge onto the word.

Repeat until all the sponges are gone! | Have them identify each shape and color. Have them paint each shape a different color. | -dish washing brush.

Sponge Toss: Outdoor Activity -bucket of water -5-10 sponges -sidewalk chalk

If you are doing this activity indoors: Write down the words on a regular sheets of paper, and place them over a plastic mat or towel to soak up water.

Shape Painting -black marker -white construction paper -blue, red ,and green washable paint |
|---|---|---|---|---|---|---|

Ocean Theme Week: 4

	Circle Time	Craft	Sensory	Gross Motor	Fine Motor	Materials Needed
Monday	Sight Word: THIS

Number of the Week :40

Color of the week: Brown

Shape Review Oval

Your Choice Book! | Shipwreck Craft!

Give your child some popsicle sticks (4)

Have them paint the popsicle sticks with brown washable paint.

Give them a paper plate and some precut blue tissue paper.

Have them glue the tissue paper inside of the plate. Make it so the entire inside area is covered.

Then have your child spread their sticks around the plate to make it look like a | Fish Egg Squish!

Unroll some bubble wrap. Place it on the floor.

Have your child close their eyes.

Have them walk slowly around the bubble wrap Make sure to hold their hands.

Tell them they are stepping on some squishy fish eggs! | Play a game of Ocean Theme Simon Says!

Walk like a Crab

Slither like an eel

Wiggle your arms like a Jellyfish | Bathtub Ocean Mural

Place your child in an empty bath tub!

Give them some washable water colors and a paintbrush.

Have them paint an ocean mural in the tub

NOTE: ALWAYS TEST WATER COLOR FIRST ON SMALL WASHABLE SURFACE TO MAKE SURE THAT IT WILL NOT STAIN TUB.

DO NOT LEAVE YOUR CHILD UNNATTENDED IN THE TUB. ALWAYS SUPERVISE YOUR CHILD TO AVOID ACCIDENT OR INJURY! | Shipwreck Craft! -paper plate -popsicle sticks (4) -washable brown paint -blue tissue paper -glue -paint brush

Fish Egg Feet Squish! -bubble wrap paper (Make sure to have them walk around slowly. Feel the bubble pop beneath their feet. HOLD THEIR HANDS. LEAD THEM AROUND! SAFETY FIRST!)

Ocean Theme Simon Says:

Just yourselves! Take turns being Simon! Recruit some friends and family members! The more the merrier! |

		shipwreck, then glue them down!				Bathtub Ocean Mural -bathtub -watercolors ALWAYS TEST WATER COLOR FIRST ON SMALL WASHABLE SURFACE TO MAKE SURE THAT IT WILL NOT STAIN TUB). DO NOT LEAVE YOUR CHILD UNNATTENDED IN THE TUB. ALWAYS SUPERVISE YOUR CHILD TO AVOID ACCIDENT OR INJURY!
Tuesday	Sight Word: THIS Number of the Week :40 Color of the week: Brown	Treasure Box! Give your child a shoe box! Have them use washable brown paint to paint the outside of the box.	Sensory Bin Fill your bin with the following: -dry pinto beans -plastic measuring cups. -plastic bowls	Number Kicks! Write down numbers 30-40 on paper/plastic cups! One number per cup! Set them up in a horizontal line.	Play Dough Shapes! Have your child form the following shapes using play dough -oval -rectangle -triangle -diamond	Treasure Box! -shoe box with lid! -gold glitter glue -brown washable paint -paint brush Sensory Bin: -plastic bin large enough to fit 3 pairs of shoes -uncooked pinto beans

| | Shape Review Oval

Your Choice Book! | After the paint has dried, have them add some streaks of gold glitter glue to the sides! | | Spread them out!

Give your child a small soccer ball. Have they maneuver the soccer ball from across the room, and then aim their kick to knock down the target cup.

Make sure they identify the number on the cup before the final kick! | -star | -plastic measuring cups
-plastic bowls

Always supervise your child when working with small objects that may pose choking hazard!

Number Kicks!
-paper/plastic cups (10)
-washable marker
-child sized soccer ball

(Best if down outside, but can also be done indoors. Just make sure to clear the area of any breakables!)

Play Dough Shapes
-play dough |
| Wednesday | Sight Word: THIS

Number of the Week :40

Color of the | Fishing Pole Craft

Punch a hole through the end of an empty paper towel roll.

Have your child use | Sensory Bottle:

Fill your sensory bottle a little more than half way with water. | Life Guard Rescue!

Place 5 stuffed animals on a towel on the floor.

Tell your child that he/she is a lifeguard. | Shell Stencils!

Give your child some crayons and a white piece of paper.

Place some shells beneath the paper.

Have your child press down on | Fishing Pole Craft
-empty paper towel roll
-white yarn
-paper clip
-brown washable paint
-paint brush

Sensory Bottle:
-plastic water bottle |

	week: Brown Shape Review Oval Your Choice Book!	brown washable paint and a paintbrush to completely cover their paper roll. This is the fishing pole! Give them a long string of white yarn. Have them thread the yarn through the hole. Help them to tie a knot so that the string is securely fastened to the roll. This is the fishing line! Give your child a paper clip. Have them tie the paper clip the end of the fishing line. This is the hook.	Next add 2-3 Drops of baby oil. Add a drop of green food coloring Add some glitter Add some sea shells (the tiny ones that are store bought). Make sure you seal it tightly before giving it to your child! You do not want a glittery spill!	They must run across the room grab a buddy and then pretend to swim back to shore, then they must drop off the buddy and go back to rescue another one. Repeat until all the buddies are back to safety!	the shells as they color over the paper! Watch the color shell shapes appear!	-glitter -baby oil -green food coloring -store bought mini shells Life Guard Rescue -5 stuffed animals -towel Shell Stencils -white paper -3 Shells (size of your palm) -crayons

| Thursday | Sight Word: THIS

Number of the Week :40

Color of the week: Brown

Shape Review Oval

Your Choice Book! | Handprint Palm Leaves

Paint the inside of your child's hand with brown washable paint.

Have stack their handprint one on top of the other to create the trunk of their palm tree.

Paint their other hand with green washable paint. Have them stamp their hand at the top of the tree trunk multiple times to create the palm leaves.

Have them dip their finger in brown washable paint to create some coconuts at the top of the tree! | Sensory Bin

Fill your bin with the following: -sand -plastic gold treasure coins! | Obstacle course!

Using painter's tape create a straight line on the floor!

Have your child pretend it is a balance beam!

Place 5 cups on the floor Make sure to leave enough room for your child to hop over them. | Colors and Words!

Tape some shelf paper to the wall. The sticky side should be facing your child.

Using red, black, green, blue, and purple, washable marker write down the following words on the paper. Make sure each word is a different color.

-THIS
-THE
-AS
-IS
-CAT

Give your child a cup of matching color fuzzy pom poms. Have them identify each word and then place the correct color pom pom on the word! | Handprint Palm Leaves -brown and green washable paint -white construction paper -paintbrush

-Sensory Bin: -plastic bin large enough to fit 3 pairs of shoes -sand -plastic pirate treasure coins (can usually be found at the dollar store).

Obstacle Course! -painter's tape -5 paper cups

Colors and Words -washable markers: red, black, green, blue, and purple

-pom poms: red, black, green, blue, and purple -tape -sticky shelf paper |
|---|---|---|---|---|---|

Friday	Sight Word: THIS	Orca Whale Craft!	Sensory Bin	Fun with Whale Spouts!	Tasty Lifeguard Tower!	Orca Whale Craft
		Precut a triangle the size of your hand using black construction paper	Fill your bin with the following:	Turn on the sprinklers!	Build a Lifeguard tower with marshmallows and pretzel sticks!	-Black and White construction paper -glue -googly eyes -empty soda bottle
	Number of the Week :40		-sand -rocks	Have your child pretend that the sprinklers are whale spouts!		
	Color of the week: Brown	This is your whale tail	-plastic shells			
		Give your child an empty soda bottle.				Sensory Bin: -plastic bin large enough to fit 3 pairs of shoes -sand -rocks -shells(plastic)
	Shape Review Oval			Have Fun Running and Jumping through the sprinklers!		
	Your Choice Book!	Have them tear some black construction paper, and glue them onto one side of the bottle.		(Safety First! Make sure the area is safe from any possible hazards, sharp objects, or things that your child can stumble on!)		Always supervise your child when playing with small items that may pose choking hazard!
		Have them tear up some white construction paper and glue the pieces to the other side of the bottle.				Fun with Whale Spouts! -sprinklers -bathing suit -water shoes -sunscreen!
		Both sides should be completely covered.				Always supervise your child. Make sure that they are comfortable and that the area is free from sharp objects or
		Have them glue a googly eye				

						things that can cause them to stumble. If it's sunny make sure to wear sunscreen! Tasty Lifeguard Tower -pretzels sticks and marshmallows Always supervise your child when working with small objects that may pose choking hazard!
		to each side of their orca whale. Note: The thicker part of the bottle is the head. Have them glue on the whale tail to the opening of the bottle.				

It has been an absolute pleasure to join you on your homeschooling journey! I hope you and your child have enjoyed the learning activities! It is now time to review everything that you have learned together. Remember, everything that is presented in this curriculum can be changed or modified to fit your child's educational needs. This includes the assessments. If your child would prefer to sing their ABC's while playing soccer then by all means allow them to do so! If you child wants to play a game of wall ball shapes then have that by their final exam. It's all about meeting the learning needs of your child. Each child is different. Each child has their own special gifts. They will learn and grow at their own pace. The great thing about homeschooling is that we are able to create tailored learning plans that will benefit our children.